W9-BYX-218

From Pumpkin Time
to Valentines

From Pumpkin Time to Valentines

Sneaking Language Arts Strategies into Holiday Celebrations

Susan Ohanian

1994
TEACHER IDEAS PRESS
A Division of
Libraries Unlimited
Englewood, Colorado

FRANKLIN PIERCE
COLLEGE LIBRARY
RINDGE, N.H. 03461

This book is dedicated to Shirley Russell,
still learning and teaching after 30+ years.

Copyright ©1994 Susan Ohanian
All Rights Reserved
Printed in the United States of America

No part of this publication may be reproduced, stored in a retrieval system, or transmitted, in any form or by any means, electronic, mechanical, photocopying, recording, or otherwise, without the prior written permission of the publisher. An exception is made for individual library media specialists and teachers who may make copies of the activity sheets for classroom use for a single school. Other portions of the book (up to 15 pages) may be copied for in-service programs or other educational programs in a single school.

TEACHER IDEAS PRESS
A Division of
Libraries Unlimited, Inc.
P.O. Box 6633
Englewood, CO 80155-6633
1-800-237-6124

Library of Congress Cataloging-in-Publication Data

Ohanian, Susan.
    From pumpkin time to valentines : sneaking language arts strategies into holiday celebrations / Susan Ohanian.
    xi, 131 p.   22x28 cm.
    Includes bibliographical references.
    ISBN 1-56308-171-7
    1. Language arts (Elementary)--United States. 2. Halloween--United States. 3. Saint Valentine's Day--United States.
    4. Activity programs in education--United States.   I. Title.
LB1576.O37 1993
372.6--dc20   93-35767
                                                          CIP

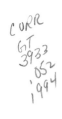
CURR
GT
3933
.O52
1994

Contents

CELEBRATE FEBRUARY: FRIENDSHIP MONTH

Acknowledgments

"Halloween," by Phyllis J. Perry. Copyright ©1971 by Scholastic *Instructor*. Used by permission of Scholastic Inc. Page 2.

"On a Dark, Dark Hill" from *Funnybones* by Alan Ahlberg. Copyright ©1981 by Alan and Janet Ahlberg. By permission of Greenwillow Books, a division of William Morrow & Company, Inc. Page 5.

"Tiptoe Through the Graveyard" from *Spook Matinee and Other Scary Poems for Kids* by George Ulrich. Copyright ©1992 by George Ulrich. Used by permission of Dell Books, a division of Bantam Doubleday Dell Publishing Group, Inc. Page 11.

Excerpt adapted and reprinted by permission of G. P. Putnam's Sons from *Halloween with Morris and Boris*. Copyright ©1975 by Bernard Wiseman. Page 23.

Excerpt from *Yuck!* by James Stevenson. Copyright ©1984 by James Stevenson. By permission of Greenwillow Books, a division of William Morrow & Company, Inc. Page 24.

"Curses!" Copyright ©1979 by Michael Patrick Hearn. Reprinted by permission of McIntosh and Otis, Inc. Page 25.

Excerpt from *Branigan's Cat and the Halloween Ghost* by Steven Kroll. Copyright ©1990 by Steven Kroll. Reprinted from *Branigan's Cat and the Halloween Ghost* by permission of Holiday House, Inc. Page. 28.

Excerpt from "Do Ghouls?" from *See My Lovely Poison Ivy* by Lilian Moore. Copyright ©1975 by Lilian Moore. Reprinted by permission of Marian Reiner for the author. Page 33.

Excerpt from *In the Haunted House* by Eve Bunting. Text copyright ©1990 by Eve Bunting. Reprinted by permission of Clarion Books/Houghton Mifflin Co. All rights reserved. Page 39.

Excerpt from *The Magic Wood* by Henry Treece. Copyright ©1992 by Henry Treece. Selection reprinted by permission of HarperCollins Publishers. Page 39.

Excerpt from *Who Can Boo the Loudest?* by Harriet Ziefert. Copyright ©1990 by Harriet Ziefert. Selection reprinted by permission of HarperCollins Publishers. Page 39.

Excerpt from *Glenda* by Janice May Udry (Trophy edition). Copyright ©1991 by Janice May Udry. Selection reprinted by permission of HarperCollins Publishers. Page 40.

Excerpt from *A Little Witch Magic* by Robert Bender. Copyright ©1992 by Robert Bender. Reprinted by permission of Henry Holt and Company, Inc. Page 40.

Excerpt from *Halloween Magic* by James W. Baker. Illustrations by George Overlie. Copyright ©1988 by Lerner Publications. Used with permission of the publisher. All rights reserved. Page 43.

Excerpt from *Ghost's Hour, Spook's Hour* by Eve Bunting. Text copyright ©1987 by Eve Bunting. Reprinted by permission of Clarion Books/Houghton Mifflin Co. All rights reserved. Page 46.

Excerpt from Samuel T. Sacket and William E. Koch, *Kansas Folklore*, University of Nebraska Press, 1961. Page 46.

"Bat" from *Halloween A B C* by Eve Merriam. Copyright ©1987 by Eve Merriam. Reprinted by permission of Marian Reiner. Page 50.

Adapted from *Within the Forest* by Susan Ohanian. Copyright ©1992 by SRA. Reprinted by permission of Science Research Associates. Page 60.

Poem from *Big and Little* by Ruth Krauss. Copyright ©1987 by Ruth Krauss. Used by permission of Scholastic Inc. Page 65.

"I Love You More Than Applesauce" from *Valentine's Day* by Jack Prelutsky. Copyright ©1983 by Jack Prelutsky. Reprinted by permission of Greenwillow Books, a division of William Morrow & Company, Inc. Page 68.

Excerpt from *Because of Lozo Brown* by Larry L. King. Copyright ©1988 by Texhouse Corporation. This material is not to be reproduced without permission from the publisher. Used by permission of Viking Penguin, a division of Penguin Books USA Inc. Page 75.

Excerpt from *Some Things Go Together* by Charlotte Zolotow. Copyright ©1969, 1983 by Charlotte Zolotow. Selection reprinted by permission of HarperCollins Publishers. Page 93.

"Going Steady" by Ian Serraillier. Copyright ©1987. Used by permission of Ian Serraillier. Page. 100.

Excerpt from *Valentine Magic* by James W. Baker. Illustrations by George Overlie. Copyright ©1988 by Lerner Publications. Used with permission of the publisher. All rights reserved. Page 102.

Introduction

Halloween and Valentine's Day are my favorite classroom celebrations. They have never been one-day affairs of sticky cupcakes and fruit punch, but a month-long celebration of language exploration. The activities in this book have grown out of two decades of helping my students experience that wonderful "Aha!" moment of discovering something new about language.

I have grouped the activities in this book around a structure that taps into pedagogical theory and plain classroom savvy. That theory is this: Emerging readers need the support of patterns; more sophisticated readers relish the cunning of puns. All children need opportunities to work independently, to read with a buddy, to use the language of favorite authors as a stimulus for their own writing, and to explore and widen their worlds through research.

Many of these activities encourage teachers and children to examine figurative language because figures of speech offer a uniquely delightful entrée into a world of inquiry that honors divergent thinking. Figurative language lessons provide opportunity for invention and play, permitting access at various levels of intellectual inquiry. The more literal thinker is not shut out from productive participation. The more creative thinker is encouraged to soar. As all children look at these old worlds in new ways, they become problem-solvers rather than answer-finders. They and their teachers learn to look at words as rich gardens of possibility and delight.

I have resisted printing an answer list for some of the puzzles in this book because of what I have learned in my own classroom. I bought a set of Elementary Science Study Creature Cards in the 1970s. These cards asked users to "choose the one that doesn't belong" by finding the common characteristics of a series of abstract figures. An answer key did not come with these cards and this meant I had to listen very carefully to the reasons my students gave for their answers. Sometimes the wrong answers were a lot more interesting than the right ones. I learned a lot about how children think. The children learned a lot about how to explain their thinking. Long years in classrooms have shown me that your students, too, will find more than one answer; and your students will offer better answers than any I could provide. So, listen up!

Halloween Happenings

Halloween

What we know today as Halloween is a shortened form of All Hallows Eve, the evening before All Hallows (All Saints') Day. It has its roots in the ancient Celtic celebration of the New Year, which occurred on November 1. On that day the Celts paid respect to Samhain, the god of the dead. The festival of Samhain was the most sacred of all Celtic celebrations because it provided a link between people and their ancestors. But it was a scary time. The Celts believed that the ghosts of their ancestors roamed the countryside, sometimes spoiling crops and causing other trouble. People put out food for the dead souls, hoping to placate them. People also put on masks and marched in parades, hoping to trick the spirits into following them out of town.

Later on, in the eighth century, the Catholic Church began to celebrate November 1st as All Saints' Day, in honor of the saints of the church. They kept many of the ancient Celtic traditions. On this day people baked pastries for the poor, who went from house to house. People also dressed up in costumes. During the Middle Ages All Saints' Day became known as All Hallow e'en, which became our Halloween.

Halloween customs spread throughout Europe. In Britain, people set carved turnips with lighted candles inside on their fences to keep evil spirits away. In Czechoslovakia, people put chairs for family spirits in front of the fireplace. In Italy, people welcomed home the souls of dead friends by leaving bread, water, and a lighted lamp on a table before going to bed. In Portugal, people went to the cemetery and ate chestnuts.

Halloween customs spread to North America. In Mexico, people celebrated Halloween by making bread and candy in the shape of a skull and crossbones or a skeleton. In the United States people were fond of practical jokes and mischief. Boys would put a farmer's gate in a tree or his wagon on the roof of the barn. Tipping over the outhouse was a popular prank.

Modern youngsters have found a more up-to-date way to celebrate Halloween. They go from house to house seeking contributions to UNICEF.

From Pumpkin Time to Valentines. Copyright 1994. Susan Ohanian. Teacher Ideas Press, P. O. Box 6633, Englewood, CO 80155.

Howling and Hissing for Halloween

Read About It

Read this poem out loud with a buddy reader.

Halloween
Phyllis J. Perry

Hooting
      Howling
            Hissing
                  Witches;

Riding
      Rasping
            Ragged
                  Switches;

Fluttering
      Frightening
            Fearsome
                  Bats;

Arching
      Awesome
            Awful
                  Cats. . . .

Write About It

1. Make a list of at least four Halloween nouns. You may choose nouns in the poem or other Halloween nouns you can think of.

2. Think of three adjectives all beginning with the same letter to describe each of your nouns. Example: Perry uses *arching, awesome,* and *awful* as adjectives to describe cats. You may also use cats in your list, if you want. But you need to come up with three different adjectives to describe your cats.

3. Finally, turn your words into a Halloween poem and read it to a friend.

From Pumpkin Time to Valentines. Copyright 1994. Susan Ohanian. Teacher Ideas Press, P. O. Box 6633, Englewood, CO 80155.

Patterns

Halloween Candy

Read this short verse about candy. It is similar to a poem by N. M. Bodecker called "Pumpkin, Pumpkin, Pumpkin Bright."

Candy,
candy,
candy sweet,
what the children
want to eat
when they
go to trick-or-treat;
candy,
candy,
candy sweet.

Write About It

Try writing a pattern of your own. If you want, you can try to create the same rhyme pattern. To help you, the rhyming lines for your pattern are starred.

Candy,

candy,

*candy_____,

_____,/

*_____,/

_____

*_____;

candy,

candy,

*candy_____.

From Pumpkin Time to Valentines. Copyright 1994. Susan Ohanian. Teacher Ideas Press, P. O. Box 6633, Englewood, CO 80155.

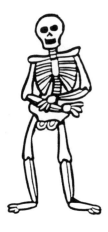

Of Snails and Slugs

Read About It

In a poem called *Witches' Menu*, Sonja Nikolay describes all the ways witches might cook lizards. Here is a poem about eating some garden inhabitants:

> Boil it, bake it, season it well,
> This is how to eat a snail.
> Mush it, stir it and add one bug,
> That is how to eat a slug.

In a poem called *Witch Pizza*, Jane Yolen says witches prefer poison ivy to anchovies on their pizzas. And in his poem *Wicked Witch's Kitchen*, X. J. Kennedy says witches eat corn on the cobweb and milkweed shakes.

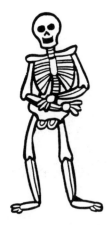

Write About It

Write your own version of a favorite food for a witch, goblin, or ghost.

From Pumpkin Time to Valentines. Copyright 1994. Susan Ohanian. Teacher Ideas Press, P. O. Box 6633, Englewood, CO 80155.

Dark Dark

Read About It

Funnybones by Janet and Allan Ahlberg starts out:

> On a dark dark hill
> There was a dark dark town.
> In the dark dark town
> there was a dark dark street.
> In the dark dark street
> there was a dark dark house.

Write About It

What do you suppose is in the dark dark house? Write about the dark dark house using the same pattern.

In the dark dark _____

was a dark dark _____.

In the dark dark _____

was a dark dark _____.

In the _____

was a _____.

In the _____

was a _____.

In the _____

was a _____.

In the _____

was a _____.

From Pumpkin Time to Valentines. Copyright 1994. Susan Ohanian. Teacher Ideas Press, P. O. Box 6633, Englewood, CO 80155.

A Very Merry Halloween

Read About It

Read this Halloween message and see if you can spot something special about the words.

A

Very
Exciting
Rousing
Yearly

Masquerade.
Exuberant
Rollicking
Riddling
Youthful

Historic
Animated
Lively
Landmark.
Ominous
Wily
Evasive
Evening.
Nightfall.

Write About It

It's your turn. Choose your own Halloween phrase, such as *A Very Merry Halloween*. Write the phrase vertically on your paper. Then turn it into a poem by writing a word or short phrase beginning with each letter. Notice in the poem above, periods help make the meaning.

From Pumpkin Time to Valentines. Copyright 1994. Susan Ohanian. Teacher Ideas Press, P. O. Box 6633, Englewood, CO 80155.

Spooky Tongue Twisters

Read About It

Read each one of these spooky tongue twisters three times as fast as you can. Then, read them to a friend.

Big black bug's blood.

Seven spooks scoop celery soup.

Great green ghosts grab gooey gummybears.

Rich witches wear ruby-red witchwatches.

Write About It

Now it's your turn! Try writing your own spooky tongue twisters.

Challenge your friends to read them three times fast.
Challenge your teacher and other adults you know to read your spooky tongue twisters.

From Pumpkin Time to Valentines. Copyright 1994. Susan Ohanian. Teacher Ideas Press, P. O. Box 6633, Englewood, CO 80155.

If I Were a Modern Halloween Witch,
Part 1

Read About It

We often see pictures on cards and in books of imaginary old-time witches stirring up potions in big black pots or riding broomsticks. An imaginary up-to-date witch might prefer to use modern technology. For example, instead of cooking in a cauldron, she might pop things into a microwave. Using the pattern below think of some ways a modern witch might differ from an old-time witch.

I WOULDN'T	*I WOULD*
I wouldn't use a cauldron.	I would use a microwave.
I wouldn't ride a broomstick.	I would
I wouldn't	I would
I wouldn't	I would
I wouldn't	I would
I wouldn't	I would

From Pumpkin Time to Valentines. Copyright 1994. Susan Ohanian. Teacher Ideas Press, P. O. Box 6633, Englewood, CO 80155.

If I Were a Modern Halloween Witch,
Part 2

Write About It

Now that you have some good ideas about how a modern Halloween witch might behave, you are ready to design a Halloween greeting card featuring this modern Halloween witch.

You may decide you want to make your card a surprise card by having moving parts in it. You may decide you want to make a lift-the-flap card—with an old-time witch on the top of the flap and the surprise modern witch underneath the flap.

1. Tape, staple, or glue a paper flap to a piece of construction paper or tagboard. Attach only the top edge of the flap. The flap may be any size. If you wish, you can make the flap in the shape of a witch.

2. You may want it to be a side flap.

3. You may decide to have more than one lift-flap on the front of your card.

Design your card—and send it to somebody who is nice to you!

From Pumpkin Time to Valentines. Copyright 1994. Susan Ohanian. Teacher Ideas Press, PO Box 6633, Englewood, CO 80155.

Dressing Up

Read About It

In *Arthur's Halloween*, when Marc Brown's popular hero Arthur goes to school on Halloween, he dresses up as Superman. His teacher is a giant robot, and the Brain is wrapped in aluminum foil. "I'm a baked potato," says the Brain.

Write About It

Write about the funniest or most amazing Halloween costume you ever wore or saw someone else wear.

From Pumpkin Time to Valentines. Copyright 1994. Susan Ohanian. Teacher Ideas Press, PO Box 6633, Englewood, CO 80155.

Scaring Ourselves

Read About It

Read this poem with a buddy reader.

Tiptoe Through the Graveyard
George Ulrich

I tiptoed through the graveyard.
I didn't make a sound.
I didn't want to wake the ghouls
Lying underground.

Just one small noise and they'd awake
And grab me by the hem.
They'd pull me down into the ground
And make me one of them. (Tra-la)

(From *The Spook Matinee and Other Scary Poems for Kids* by George Ulrich.)

Write About It

Make a list of scary things.

Write about how you feel about
one scary thing on your list.

Extra Credit

Take a poll of your classmates. What scares people in your class the most?

From Pumpkin Time to Valentines. Copyright 1994. Susan Ohanian. Teacher Ideas Press, PO Box 6633, Englewood, CO 80155.

Sleep Well

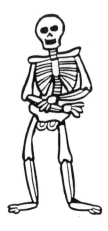

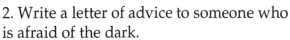

Read About It

In "Advice on How to Sleep Well Halloween Night" in *Best Witches*, Jane Yolen says to hang garlic over your bed before you go to sleep to keep you safe.

Think About It

1. When you have trouble sleeping, what do you do?

2. Write a letter of advice to someone who is afraid of the dark.

From Pumpkin Time to Valentines. Copyright 1994. Susan Ohanian. Teacher Ideas Press, PO Box 6633, Englewood, CO 80155.

Ghoulish Recipes

| Read About It |

Here are some Halloween treats you might find at a haunted house:

poison ivy greens   corn-on-the-cobweb
ghoulash   french flies
ghoulade   slime lime pie
rotten candy   chocolate eek-clairs

| Write About It |

Now it's your turn. Write your own list of spooky Halloween treats.

Here are a few hints to help you get started. How could you transform the following words into spooky foods by changing the spelling?

spaghetti_____   blueberries_____

baloney_____   sandwiches_____

cream cheese_____   roast beef_____

Think of some more spooky foods:

From Pumpkin Time to Valentines. Copyright 1994. Susan Ohanian. Teacher Ideas Press, PO Box 6633, Englewood, CO 80155.

Ghostly Treats

Read About It

Here are some food names taken from a cookbook. Read the list with a buddy reader and change them to become good fare for ghosts and other Halloween creatures.

CAKES

Angel Food

Banana Upside-down

Black Forest Cherry

Chocolate Chip Chiffon

Triple Fudge

Lady Baltimore

Devil's Food

Tutti-Frutti

COOKIES

Chocolate Chip

Oatmeal

Peanut butter

PUDDINGS

Bread

Butterscotch

Prune Whip

Rice

Tapioca

Jell-O™

PIES

Apple

Berry

Pumpkin

Shoofly

Extra Credit

Check out a cookbook from the library. Add foods to your list.

From Pumpkin Time to Valentines. Copyright 1994. Susan Ohanian. Teacher Ideas Press, PO Box 6633, Englewood, CO 80155.

Spooky Pets

Think About It

A ghoulish household might well have some unusual pets. Horseflies, mosquitoes, earwigs, praying mantises, and tarantulas are possibilities. Make a list of some other ghoulish pets.

Extra Credit

Write a newspaper ad—either a Want Ad or a Lost and Found about a ghoulish pet.

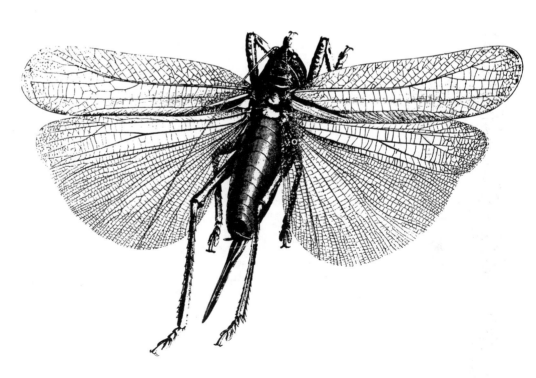

From Pumpkin Time to Valentines. Copyright 1994. Susan Ohanian. Teacher Ideas Press, PO Box 6633, Englewood, CO 80155.

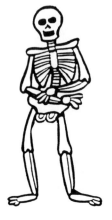

A Garden of Frightful Flowers

Talk About It

Ask six friends to name their favorite flowers. Make a list.

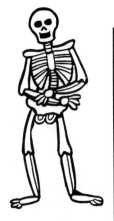

Read About It

Halloween ghouls and goblins might admire different flowers and plants.

Bachelor's button	Devil's paintbrush	Rattlesnake master
Black-eyed Susan	Devil's tongue	Skunkweed
Bleeding heart	Dogtooth violet	Sneezeweed
Bluebonnet	Elephant-ear fern	Spanish dagger
Blue-eyed grass	Fleabane	Spider lily
Boneset	Lion's-ear	Sweet William Catchfly
Butterfly weed	Liverleaf	Tiger lily
Cattail	Milkweed	Turtlehead
Cowslip	Mosquito trap	Witchweed
Crow toe	Mouse-ear	Yellow loosestrife

Write About It

Using some of these flower names, and any others you might find in a gardening encyclopedia or other reference book, create a Halloween garden. You may write a poem, write a seed order, or draw a picture of the garden.

From Pumpkin Time to Valentines. Copyright 1994. Susan Ohanian. Teacher Ideas Press, PO Box 6633, Englewood, CO 80155.

Things to Do Today

Read About It

You can invent some interesting spooky adventures for a ghost, a ghoul, or a skeleton. For example, a ghost might go shopping at Spooks "R" Us, go to the scaredressers, or meet a ghoulfriend in Witchita.

Write About It

Fill in this schedule for your favorite spooky creature.

THINGS TO DO TODAY/TONIGHT

Date_____ Completed

1) _Play hide-and-go-shriek_ ☐

2) _____ ☐

3) _____ ☐

4) _____ ☐

5) _____ ☐

6) _____ ☐

7) _____ ☐

8) _____ ☐

9) _____ ☐

10) _____ ☐

From Pumpkin Time to Valentines. Copyright 1994. Susan Ohanian. Teacher Ideas Press, PO Box 6633, Englewood, CO 80155.

Ghastly Goodies

Read About It

The Wacky Book of Witches by Annie Civardi and Graham Philpot has lots of foods eaten by witches, including:

Mice Krispies	Shredded worms	Mayonnose
Lemmingade	Heartichokes	Paincakes and Chokealot sauce

Poets also like to write about things witches and other Halloween creatures might eat. Check your library to see if you can find a Halloween food poem. Read it to at least three friends.

Write About It

Take an imaginary ghoulfriend for a Halloween lunch. Fill out this sales slip with your ghoulish treats. (Hint: how about skunk cabbage for an appetizer?)

Guest Check

PLEASE PAY CASHIER

PORTIONS	ITEM	AMOUNT
	TAX	

CHECK NO.	GUESTS	TABLE	ATTENDANT	TOTAL
9313				

5K 800 REDIFORM   ORIGINAL

Alternative

You may want to design the restaurant menu.

From Pumpkin Time to Valentines. Copyright 1994. Susan Ohanian. Teacher Ideas Press, PO Box 6633, Englewood, CO 80155.

The Perfect Halloween Snack

Write About It

Write the recipe for making a toothsome Halloween treat.

First, put 2 cups _____ in a bowl.

Add 1 teaspoon _____ and 1/2 teaspoon _____.

Stir in 1 cup _____.

Cook over low flame until _____.

Add 1/2 chopped _____.

Add 3 _____.

Spread on _____.

Serves: _____.

The name of this treat is: _____.

From Pumpkin Time to Valentines. Copyright 1994. Susan Ohanian. Teacher Ideas Press, P. O. Box 6633, Englewood, CO 80155.

Nickelodeon Slime

Read About It

Here's the recipe for Nickelodeon slime. According to Daniella Burr, the author of *Don't Just Sit There! 50 Ways to Have a Nickelodeon Day*, "The real Nickelodeon slime can't be owned. Like other great natural resources, the mysterious substance comes directly from the center of the earth. Top scientists are still baffled and are unable to explain this bizarre, living, green, gooey mineral!"

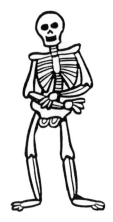

But in that same book they give a recipe so you can make your own version of Nickelodeon slime:

1. Cook a batch of instant oatmeal but add twice the amount of water the directions call for.

2. Mix in green food coloring (the amount depends on how green you want your slime).

3. Stir until all the oatmeal is green.

4. Cool.

Make a List

What are the possible uses of this slime?

From Pumpkin Time to Valentines. Copyright 1994. Susan Ohanian. Teacher Ideas Press, P. O. Box 6633, Englewood, CO 80155.

A Monster Meal

Think About It

Invite a monster, ghost, ghoul or other creature of your choice to lunch. List the foods you both eat on this guest check.

Guest Check

PLEASE PAY CASHIER

PORTIONS	ITEM	AMOUNT
	TAX	

CHECK NO.	GUESTS	TABLE	ATTENDANT	TOTAL
9313				

5K 800 REDIFORM   ORIGINAL

From Pumpkin Time to Valentines. Copyright 1994. Susan Ohanian. Teacher Ideas Press, P. O. Box 6633, Englewood, CO 80155.

Bewitching Riddles

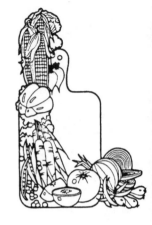

Read About It

What does a witch eat on Halloween?

    Corn-on-the-cobweb?
    Ghoulash?
    Ghoulade?

Write About It

Work with a buddy reader/writer to come up with some witch-ly riddles. Here are some questions to help you get started.

1. Where does a witch eat?

2. What does a witch eat?

3. What cities does a witch visit?

4. What books does a witch read?

5. What is a witch's favorite TV show?

6. How does a witch like to spend her leisure time?

From Pumpkin Time to Valentines. Copyright 1994. Susan Ohanian. Teacher Ideas Press, P. O. Box 6633, Englewood, CO 80155.

Say What You Mean

Read About It

Read this scene from *Halloween with Morris and Boris* by Bernard Wiseman with a buddy reader.

Boris: Hooray! Halloween is here.

Morris: Halloween is not here.
          I don't see him.

Boris: Halloween is not a him.
          Halloween is a . . .

Morris: I know!
          Halloween is a her.

Boris: No!
          Halloween is a holiday.
          It is when
          children make pumpkins. . . .

Morris: Children can't make pumpkins.
          Pumpkins grow.

Directions
1. Explain the language problem.

2. Write another scene in which Morris misunderstands something about Halloween, such as candycorn.

From Pumpkin Time to Valentines. Copyright 1994. Susan Ohanian. Teacher Ideas Press, P. O. Box 6633, Englewood, CO 80155.

Brewing Magic Potions

Read About It

Read this scene from *Yuck!* by James Stevenson with a buddy reader, and write your own play.

> Audience 1: What is that gross, disgusting smell?
>
> Audience 2: Dolores and Lavinia are brewing magic potions again!
>
> Dolores: A pinch more powdered rat tail!
>
> Lavinia: Don't forget the shark snout!
>
> Dolores: Oh, it's foul, Lavinia!
>
> Lavinia: Stencheroo, Dolores!
>
> Dolores: Let's make it even stronger, Lavinia!
>
> Lavinia: Here's more scallions and skunk cabbage!

Talk About It

Continue the conversation. What can you add to this gross, disgusting magic potion?

Note that James Stevenson invented a word: *Stencheroo*. You won't find stencheroo in a dictionary, but you don't need a dictionary to figure out what it means, do you?

Challenge

Invent two words of your own that Lavinia or Dolores might use.

From Pumpkin Time to Valentines. Copyright 1994. Susan Ohanian. Teacher Ideas Press, P. O. Box 6633, Englewood, CO 80155.

Curses!

Read About It

Read Michael Patrick Hearn's two-part poem with a buddy reader.

Curses!

First Witch:
Ragwort, tansy, parsley, pea!
    You'd better stay away from me!
Purple pumpkins, crabgrass green!
    You're the ugliest thing I've ever seen!
Bumble,
Grumble,
Mumblety peg!
Let a worm crawl up your leg!
Brooklyn needle,
Jersey pin!
Let a snail sit on your chin!
    Nyeh!

Second Witch:
Oh, pickle water!
Penguin toes!
Let your nose grow like a gardenia grows!
Six times six,
And two times two!
    Let your hair turn blue!
    Let your hair turn blue!
    Let it stick like glue!
And if you think that's bad,
    If you think that's bad,
    If you think *that's* bad,
Here's something worse:
You'll never get free of *my* witch's curse!
    So there!

Write About It

Now it's your turn. You and your buddy reader make up your own curses. Here are some words that may help you get started: broccoli, pea soup, liver, camel humps, ostrich ears, mustard, and Cincinnati. Use these words if you like, and think up some more funny curse words of your own. Write a two-part curse poem with your buddy reader. Read it to some friends.

From Pumpkin Time to Valentines. Copyright 1994. Susan Ohanian. Teacher Ideas Press, P. O. Box 6633, Englewood, CO 80155.

Scary Things

Read About It

Linda Williams's book *The Little Old Lady Who Was Not Afraid of Anything* begins:

Once upon a time,
there was a little old lady who was not afraid of anything!

Talk About It

Interview three people and find out what scares them.
If you interview adults, you may want to ask what scared them when they were your age or you may want to ask them what scares them now.

1.

2.

3.

Make a graph of what scares your class the most.

From Pumpkin Time to Valentines. Copyright 1994. Susan Ohanian. Teacher Ideas Press, P. O. Box 6633, Englewood, CO 80155.

What About Bats?

| Read About It |

Read this bat passage below to three adults. Then interview them. Ask them if they have any bat stories or any opinions about bats.

Do You Know:
In some parts of the world bats are considered lucky. In China and Poland they are good luck omens. To the Chinese, in fact, the bat stands for long life and happiness. In Britain, some people think that fair weather is coming if you see a bat flying.

(from *Weird! The Complete Book of Halloween Words* by Peter Limburg.)

Adult 1

Adult 2

Adult 3

From Pumpkin Time to Valentines. Copyright 1994. Susan Ohanian. Teacher Ideas Press, P. O. Box 6633, Englewood, CO 80155.

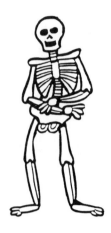

Superstitions, Part 1

Read About It

Read the passage below to three people.

Branigan's Cat and the Halloween Ghost
Steven Kroll

John Branigan was a poor woodcutter. He lived in a small hut near a dark forest. All he had in the world was a black cat called Llewellyn.

Llewellyn looked fierce, but he was really very gentle. He loved curling up in Branigan's lap. When Branigan scratched him behind the ears, he purred.

Branigan loved his cat so much that when he went into the village to sell his wood, he took Llewellyn with him. But each time the villagers saw how big the cat was and how fierce he looked, they fled to their homes in fear. Even the bravest knew black cats could bring bad luck.

Find Out

Ask the people to whom you read the passage if they are superstitious about black cats or anything else.

Person 1

Person 2

Person 3

From Pumpkin Time to Valentines. Copyright 1994. Susan Ohanian. Teacher Ideas Press, P. O. Box 6633, Englewood, CO 80155.

Superstitions, Part 2

Read About It

Here are some old superstitions. Read them and see what you think. Then read them to three other people. See if you can find someone who has heard of some of these superstitions. Find out if they know any more you can share with your class.

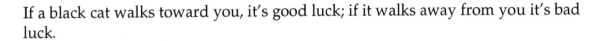

Some People Think . . .

If a black cat walks toward you, it's good luck; if it walks away from you it's bad luck.

If you spit on your fishhook, the fish will bite.

If you spit on your hands before entering the arena, you'll be lucky in a fight.

Wearing eyeshadow protects you from the Evil Eye.

The number of times you can pop your knuckles equals the number of persons of the opposite sex who love you.

If you kill a spider, you'll have bad luck until you've killed 53 flies.

Spilling salt is unlucky unless you quickly throw a pinch over your left shoulder.

Climbing a ladder with an odd number of rungs is very lucky.

Walking under a ladder is very unlucky.

From Pumpkin Time to Valentines. Copyright 1994. Susan Ohanian. Teacher Ideas Press, P. O. Box 6633, Englewood, CO 80155.

Halloween Traditions

Interview three adults over 50 years old. Ask them to tell you about Halloween traditions they remember from their youth.

Interviewee 1

Interviewee 2

Interviewee 3

From Pumpkin Time to Valentines. Copyright 1994. Susan Ohanian. Teacher Ideas Press, P. O. Box 6633, Englewood, CO 80155.

Sticks and Stones

Read About It

When the little witch Nesta goes to the School for Spells in *Nesta the Little Witch*, her teacher's name is Windbag Wartnose, and she enjoys giving the little witch students long, complicated, witchy things to learn. In *Lulu Goes to Witch School*, the teacher's name is Miss Slime.

Think About It

1. Make up some spooky names.

2. Make up some spooky school homework.

3. Draw a picture of a spooky lunchbox.

From Pumpkin Time to Valentines. Copyright 1994. Susan Ohanian. Teacher Ideas Press, P. O. Box 6633, Englewood, CO 80155.

The Names of Things

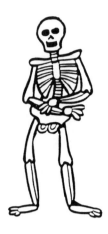

Read About It

If you took a peek at the books on the shelves in the rooms of Dracula's children, you might see these titles: *Moldylocks and the Three Bats, Charlie and the Batwing Factory,* and *Where the Wild Things Are.*

Think About It

Can you think of some other books these children might like? Make a list.

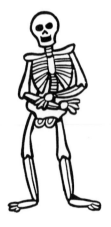

How about TV shows and movies? What would be their favorite shows?

Extra Challenge

Design the front page of the Dracula family newspaper.

From Pumpkin Time to Valentines. Copyright 1994. Susan Ohanian. Teacher Ideas Press, P. O. Box 6633, Englewood, CO 80155.

Ghoulish Matters

Read About It

Read this poem to a friend.

Do Ghouls?
Lilian Moore

Do ghouls
go out
on a rainy day?

When it
splishes and
sploshes,
do ghouls
wear ghoul-oshes?

Think About It

Lilian Moore has made a pun with *ghoul*. She writes "ghoul-oshes" instead of "galoshes." Can you think of other words you might pun with ghoul?

Hint: How about a sweet drink?
How about a female friend?

Challenge

There are also some pun possibilities with "ghost." "Ghost-toasties" is one that comes up in riddles. Can you think of any more?

Once you have your puns for ghoul and ghost you will be well on your way to writing some Halloween riddles.

From Pumpkin Time to Valentines. Copyright 1994. Susan Ohanian. Teacher Ideas Press, P. O. Box 6633, Englewood, CO 80155.

Check That Broom Closet

Think About It

Here are some ordinary objects that take on extraordinary meaning when you turn them into monster riddles. You may have to change the spelling of a few to make them work. Others are fine, as is.

1. a broom closet

2. masking tape

3. blood bank

4. petrified wood

5. evaporated milk

6. Lake Erie

7. discount store

8. bathrobe

9. blood cells

10. blood hound

11. bathtub

12. badminton

13. horoscope

14. Wichita, Kansas

15. ragtime

From Pumpkin Time to Valentines. Copyright 1994. Susan Ohanian. Teacher Ideas Press, P. O. Box 6633, Englewood, CO 80155.

Looking at Language

How Do You Feel?

Think About It

Sometimes we say we have "butterflies in our stomach." Ghosts and goblins, witches and werewolves might say they have "bats in their stomach." Change these popular idioms to ghoulish expressions. Sometimes the idiom is already well suited to a witch.

1. so hungry he could eat a horse
2. eat like a bird
3. not my cup of tea
4. cry over spilled milk
5. cool as a cucumber
6. cat got your tongue
7. put a bug in his ear
8. a frog in one's throat
9. a bee in one's bonnet
10. that's the way the cookie crumbles
11. feeling on top of the world
12. pleased as punch
13. I'll eat my hat
14. a meat-and-potatoes sort of person
15. nutty as a fruitcake
16. a heart of gold

Extra Credit

Turn your new idiom into a Halloween riddle.

Example: What did the witch say when her daughter was upset?
(There's no use crying over spilled rat poison.)
What did the vampire say when his son was upset?
(There's no use crying over spilled blood.)

From Pumpkin Time to Valentines. Copyright 1994. Susan Ohanian. Teacher Ideas Press, P. O. Box 6633, Englewood, CO 80155.

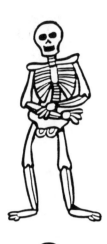

Lots to Chew On

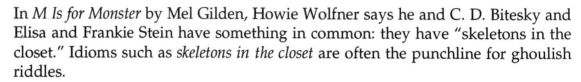

Think About It

In *M Is for Monster* by Mel Gilden, Howie Wolfner says he and C. D. Bitesky and Elisa and Frankie Stein have something in common: they have "skeletons in the closet." Idioms such as *skeletons in the closet* are often the punchline for ghoulish riddles.

Example: What happened when Count Dracula did his spring housecleaning? (He found the skeletons in his closet.)

1. Try writing your own riddles using at least three of the following idioms. Try your riddles out on a buddy reader.

being a pain in the neck

getting your teeth into something

working the skeleton crew

two heads are better than one

having bats in the belfry

lending someone a hand

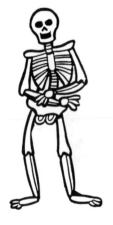

going to bat for him

having a bone to pick with someone

coming apart at the seams

at the cutting edge

Note: Mel Gilden's Fifth Grade Monster series is published by Avon and is filled with these kinds of jokes.

From Pumpkin Time to Valentines. Copyright 1994. Susan Ohanian. Teacher Ideas Press, P. O. Box 6633, Englewood, CO 80155.

Lend Me a Hand

Think About It

Here are some idioms with special meaning for ghosts and ghouls and other creatures that go bump in the night. Try your hand at turning these into ghoulish riddles. Find a buddy reader to lend a hand.

1. Why don't you zip up your lip?

2. He's a real bonehead.

3. Could you lend me a hand?

4. He'll talk your ear off.

5. You've opened a real can of worms.

6. I always say, two heads are better than one.

7. I'm all tied up right now.

8. They don't have a ghost of a chance of winning the game.

Extra Credit

Illustrate your riddles.

From Pumpkin Time to Valentines. Copyright 1994. Susan Ohanian. Teacher Ideas Press, P. O. Box 6633, Englewood, CO 80155.

Not in Vain

Think About It

Here are some more idioms to turn into super ghoulish riddles.

1. to love in vain.

2. to have tired blood

3. to live on next to nothing

4. to bat an eye

5. to have a lot at stake

6. to fly off the handle

7. to have grave doubts

8. a splitting headache

9. bats in the belfry

10. all wrapped up

From Pumpkin Time to Valentines. Copyright 1994. Susan Ohanian. Teacher Ideas Press, P. O. Box 6633, Englewood, CO 80155.

How Does It Begin? Part 1

Read About It

Sometimes authors try to grab the reader with the very first sentence. Read the following opening paragraphs, and decide which one "grabs" you the most. Which one do you like the best?

A.　　　　　　　This is the house where the scary ones hide,
　　　　　　　Open the door and step softly inside.
　　　　　　　An organ is playing a funeral air.
　　　　　　　It's playing and playing, but nobody's there.

(Excerpt from Eve Bunting, *In the Haunted House.*)

B.　　　　　　　Two ghosts met in the moonlight.
　　　　　　　"Who can boo the loudest?" asked the big ghost.
　　　　　　　"I can!" said the little one.
　　　　　　　"No, I can!" said the big one.
　　　　　　　"Let's have a booing contest," said the little ghost.

(Excerpt from Harriet Ziefert, *Who Can Boo the Loudest?* illustrated by Claire Schumacher.)

C.　This last one is not a story but the opening part of a poem.
　　　　　　　The wood is full of shining eyes,
　　　　　　　The wood is full of creeping feet,
　　　　　　　The wood is full of tiny cries:
　　　　　　　You must not go to the wood at night!

(Excerpt from Henry Treece, *The Magic Wood*, illustrated by Barry Moser.)

Think About It

1. Which one of these books would you like to read more of? Why?

2. Does one selection seem scarier than others? How does the author make it scary?

3. Make a list of 10 things you think are scary. Compare your list with a friend's list.

From Pumpkin Time to Valentines. Copyright 1994. Susan Ohanian. Teacher Ideas Press, P. O. Box 6633, Englewood, CO 80155.

How Does It Begin? Part 2

| Read About It |

Sometimes authors try to grab the reader with the very first sentence. Read the following opening paragraphs and decide which one "grabs" you the most. Which one do you like the best?

A. Broomhelga had a reputation as the meanest witch in town. Everyone was afraid to walk down her street. Everyone, that is, except for one little girl named Wanda. Secretly, she was curious.

(Excerpt from Robert Bender, *A Little Witch Magic*.)

B. Like most witches, Glenda Glinka could change herself into almost anything she wanted to be. She had recently been a rabbit, a bear, a snake, and an umbrella. Changing herself was her favorite amusement—her hobby you might say. Although Glenda Glinka often used magic, no one had ever caught her using it. She was too clever a witch for that.

(Excerpt from Janice May Udry, *Glenda*, illustrated by Marc Simont.)

C. When I woke up it was really dark. Something went Woooooo outside my window. "Don't be scared," I told myself. "It's just the wind." I slid out of bed.

(Excerpt from Eve Bunting, *Ghost's Hour, Spook's Hour*.)

| Think About It |

1. Do any of these excerpts sound scary? How does the author's language make you think this?

2. Do any of these excerpts sound funny? How does the author's language make you think this?

3. What do you think might happen next in each story?

From Pumpkin Time to Valentines. Copyright 1994. Susan Ohanian. Teacher Ideas Press, P. O. Box 6633, Englewood, CO 80155.

Take a Poll

Read About It

According to *Halloween Holiday Grab Bag* by Judith Stamper these are the twenty top costume ideas.

Black cat
Devil
Fortuneteller/gypsy
Ghost
Monster
Movie star
Mummy
Nerd
Outer-space creature
Pirate
Pumpkin
Robot
Rock star
Skeleton
Super-hero or super-heroine
Vampire or vampirella
Werewolf
Witch
Wizard
Zombie

Take a Poll

What is the most popular costume idea in your classroom? Ask your classmates. Report your findings in a graph.

From Pumpkin Time to Valentines. Copyright 1994. Susan Ohanian. Teacher Ideas Press, P. O. Box 6633, Englewood, CO 80155.

Phenomenal Pumpkin

| Read About It |

In 1984, Howard Dill, the Pumpkin King of Canada, grew a 493½ pound pumpkin.

| Think About It |

What could you do with a pumpkin that weighs nearly five hundred pounds? Try to come up with at least eight suggestions.

From Pumpkin Time to Valentines. Copyright 1994. Susan Ohanian. Teacher Ideas Press, P. O. Box 6633, Englewood, CO 80155.

Add It Up

Read About It

Here's some tricky Halloween math called *The Ghost Solves a Mystery*.

Offer a challenge:

1. Challenge your friend to choose any page above 99 in a mystery book. Your friend should write that number on a piece of paper when you aren't looking.

2. Your friend should choose any line among the first 9 lines on that page and write down the number of the line.

3. Then your friend should choose a word in that line among the first 9 words, counting left to right. Your friend should write down the number of the words and the word itself.

4. Ask your friend to multiply the page number by 2, multiply the result by 5, and add 20. Add the sum to the line number. Take that sum and add 5, multiply the result by 10, and add the number of the word on the line.

5. When your friend has finished the math, ask for a final answer.

6. You page through the mystery book and write something on a piece of paper. It is the word your friend selected.

How can you do it?

To find that word, you take your friend's result (a five-digit number) and subtract 250. The first three numbers of your five-digit number tell you the page of the word your friend selected. The next digit tells you what line that word is on. The last digit tells you the place of the word on the line.

(From *Halloween Magic* by James Baker.)

From Pumpkin Time to Valentines. Copyright 1994. Susan Ohanian. Teacher Ideas Press, P. O. Box 6633, Englewood, CO 80155.

What a Trip

Think About It

Here are some examples of real places in the United States with spooky names.

Witch Water Pocket, Arizona
Tombstone, Arizona
Mummy Pass, Colorado
Cape Fear, North Carolina
Skeleton Springs, South Dakota
Death Valley, California

Check It Out

Look in an atlas to see how many other spooky place names you can come up with.

Draw a map of the United States of Ghouls.

Extra Credit

Write a Chamber of Commerce tourist pamphlet for one of these places.

From Pumpkin Time to Valentines. Copyright 1994. Susan Ohanian. Teacher Ideas Press, P. O. Box 6633, Englewood, CO 80155.

Name That Place

Think About It

Some place names can be turned into spooky names.

    Examples: Washington becomes Witchington.
              Lake Erie becomes Lake Eerie.

When making these changes, it is important to listen to the sound of the name. See how many eerie place names you can invent.

Write About It

Turn at least two of your inventions into riddles.

From Pumpkin Time to Valentines. Copyright 1994. Susan Ohanian. Teacher Ideas Press, P. O. Box 6633, Englewood, CO 80155.

Tall Tale Pumpkin

Read About It

Here is a Kansas tall tale by S. T. Sacket and William Koch about a phenomenal pumpkin.

> Think of the Kansas pumpkins! Gentlemen, when I was on a farm in that glorious country I once lost three valuable cows. For three weeks I searched for them in vain and was returning home in disgust when I suddenly heard the tinkle of a cowbell. Investigation showed that the cows were inside a pumpkin, eating calmly and enjoying their commodious quarters. How did they get in you say? Well, the pumpkin vines grew rapidly there, and dragged a pumpkin over the rough ground until a hole was worn in the side, through which the cows entered. I afterwards had it cured and used it for a wagon shed.

Read More About It

If you enjoy tall tales, try the McBroom stories by Sid Fleischman.

Write About It

Try writing your own tall tale about pumpkins or anything else you choose.

From Pumpkin Time to Valentines. Copyright 1994. Susan Ohanian. Teacher Ideas Press, P. O. Box 6633, Englewood, CO 80155.

Boning Up on Your Body

√ Did you know you have about 305 bones when you are born but only 206 when you are an adult? Find out what happened to those bones!

√ Do you know what is the hardest bone in your body? Find out!

√ Do you know how many bones are in your hand? Find out!

Research It

Find out at least three more fascinating facts about your bones.

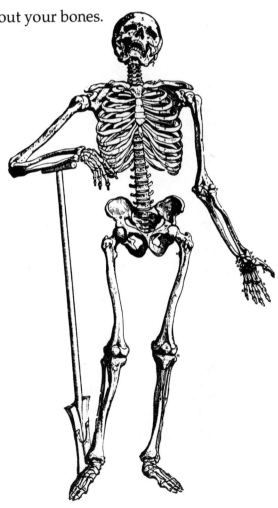

From Pumpkin Time to Valentines. Copyright 1994. Susan Ohanian. Teacher Ideas Press, P. O. Box 6633, Englewood, CO 80155.

Looking at Bats

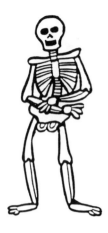

Read About It

About 30 kinds of bats live in the United States. Bats live nearly everywhere in the world. Worldwide, there are somewhere between 1,000 and 2,000 kinds of bats. They vary in size. The smallest bats have a wingspan of just two inches (5 cm), the largest have a wingspan of more than five feet (150 cm).

Little Known Bat Facts

Most bats are dark but fruit bats are brownish yellow; two South American bats are white, a variety of chin-leaf bat is bright orange, and the Indian painted bat is deep orange with black spots on its wings. Some people say it looks like a giant butterfly.

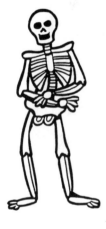

Research It

Find at least one more bat fact. (Suggestion: Are they really blind?)

Draw It

Amaze your friends! Try drawing a bat with a five-foot wing span.

From Pumpkin Time to Valentines. Copyright 1994. Susan Ohanian. Teacher Ideas Press, P. O. Box 6633, Englewood, CO 80155.

Name That Bat

Think About It

Bats have some interesting and unusual names. Read this list of names:

Ghost Bat
Fruit Bat
Bulldog Bat
Horseshoe Bat
Flying Fox Bat
Vampire Bat
Spear-Nosed Bat

Draw It

Draw three of these bats. You can draw a fanciful bat, according to what the names suggest, or you can research the bats and draw an accurate picture.

Note

Amazing Bats by Frank Greenaway, in the Eyewitness Junior series, has spectacular bat photographs as well as interesting information. It will tell you what bats like to snack on as well as where they like to live and which ones have funny faces.

From Pumpkin Time to Valentines. Copyright 1994. Susan Ohanian. Teacher Ideas Press, P. O. Box 6633, Englewood, CO 80155.

Bat Poem

Read About It

Bat
Eve Merriam

Bats in the belfry
lurk on high.
When midnight chimes,
shadows fly.

Umbrella wings,
beware, beware.
A silent swoop,
a cobwebby scare,
a rush in the darkness,
a brush against your hair.

Shiver and tremble
and don't dare shriek;
the creatures can tell
if you're faint or weak.

By dawn they're back
in their dim dank lair
up in the rafters:
waiting, waiting there.

(From *Halloween ABC* by Eve Merriam.)

Think About It

1. How do you think this poet feels about bats? Does she like them? Give evidence from the poem to support your opinion.

2. Change six words in the poem to give it the opposite feeling.

3. Read both poems to two friends and see what they think.

From Pumpkin Time to Valentines. Copyright 1994. Susan Ohanian. Teacher Ideas Press, P. O. Box 6633, Englewood, CO 80155.

Picture Your Bones, Part 1

Directions: Working with a partner, draw the outline of each other's body on butcher paper or another large piece of paper. Once you have the body outlines, draw in the bones. You can find reference books in the library to help you.

Once you have drawn the bones, you can learn the words to "Dry Bones." For a real challenge, substitute Latin or Greek terms for the everyday bone names. For example:

"The phalanges're connected to the metatarsals.
The metatarsals're connected to the tarsals.
The tarsals're connected to the tibia.
The tibia's connected to the femur.
The femur's connected to the pelvis.
The pelvis is connected to the vertebrae.
The vertebrae're connected to the skull."

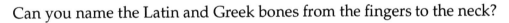

| Challenge |

Can you name the Latin and Greek bones from the fingers to the neck?

From Pumpkin Time to Valentines. Copyright 1994. Susan Ohanian. Teacher Ideas Press, P. O. Box 6633, Englewood, CO 80155.

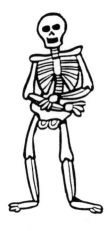

Picture Your Bones, Part 2

| Write About It |

Make a list of bony words that go with your skeleton.

| Read About It |

Find a skeleton poem in the library. Read it to a friend.

Poem title:

Poet's name:

List some of the bony words in the poem:

Are there any you especially like?

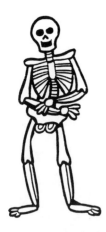

How about you? Can you write a bony poem?

From Pumpkin Time to Valentines. Copyright 1994. Susan Ohanian. Teacher Ideas Press, P. O. Box 6633, Englewood, CO 80155.

Boning Up on Skeletons

Directions

This bony fellow was drawn in the 19th century. You can get lessons on how to draw a skeleton by studying two books. In Ed Emberley's *Big Orange Drawing Book,* the author gives step-by-step directions. In *How to Draw and Color Monsters,* Don Bolognese and Elaine Raphael also give advice on how to bone up on skeleton art. The methods in these two books will definitely show you that all skeletons are not alike. One interesting thing you will see is neither skeleton has the correct number of ribs.

How about you? Can you draw a skeleton? How many ribs will you give your skeleton?

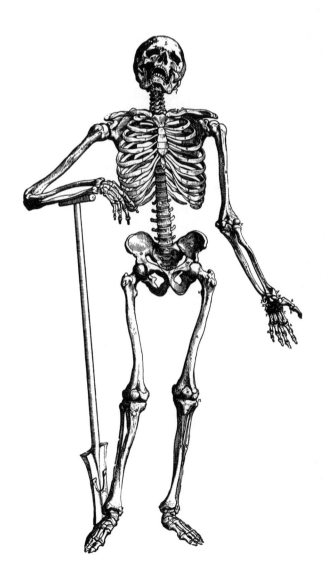

From Pumpkin Time to Valentines. Copyright 1994. Susan Ohanian. Teacher Ideas Press, P. O. Box 6633, Englewood, CO 80155.

Graphically Speaking

Directions: If you follow these directions, you will create a popular Halloween figure. Use the grid on page 55 for this fun drawing.

1. Starting at the dot on the bottom line, draw a line up one square.
2. Draw to left two squares.
3. Draw up one square.
4. Draw to left two squares.
5. Draw up one square.
6. Draw to left one square.
7. Draw up one square.
8. Draw to left one square.
9. Draw up one square.
10. Draw to left one square.
11. Draw up one square.
12. Draw to left one square.
13. Draw up two squares.
14. Draw to left one square.
15. Draw up nine squares.
16. Draw to right one square.
17. Draw up three squares.
18. Draw to right one square.
19. Draw up two squares.
20. Draw to right one square.
21. Draw up two squares.
22. Draw to right one square.
23. Draw up one square.
24. Draw to right one square.
25. Draw up one square.
26. Draw to right three squares.
27. Draw up one square.
28. Draw to right four squares.
29. Draw up five squares.
30. Draw to right two squares.
31. Draw down five squares.
32. Draw to right four squares.
33. Draw down one square.
34. Draw to right three squares.
35. Draw down one square.
36. Draw to right one square.
37. Draw down one square.
38. Draw to right one square.
39. Draw down two squares.
40. Draw to right one square.
41. Draw down two squares.
42. Draw to right one square.
43. Draw down three squares.
44. Draw to right one square.
45. Draw down nine squares.
46. Draw to left one square.
47. Draw down two squares.
48. Draw to left one square.
49. Draw down one square.
50. Draw to left one square.
51. Draw down one square.
52. Draw to left one square.
53. Draw down one square.
54. Draw to left one square.
55. Draw down one square.
56. Draw to left two squares.
57. Draw down one square.
58. Draw to left two squares.
59. Draw down one square.
60. Draw to left nine squares.
61. Decorate your design.

Challenge

Write directions so a Halloween buddy can draw a new Halloween figure you have created.

From Pumpkin Time to Valentines. Copyright 1994. Susan Ohanian. Teacher Ideas Press, P. O. Box 6633, Englewood, CO 80155.

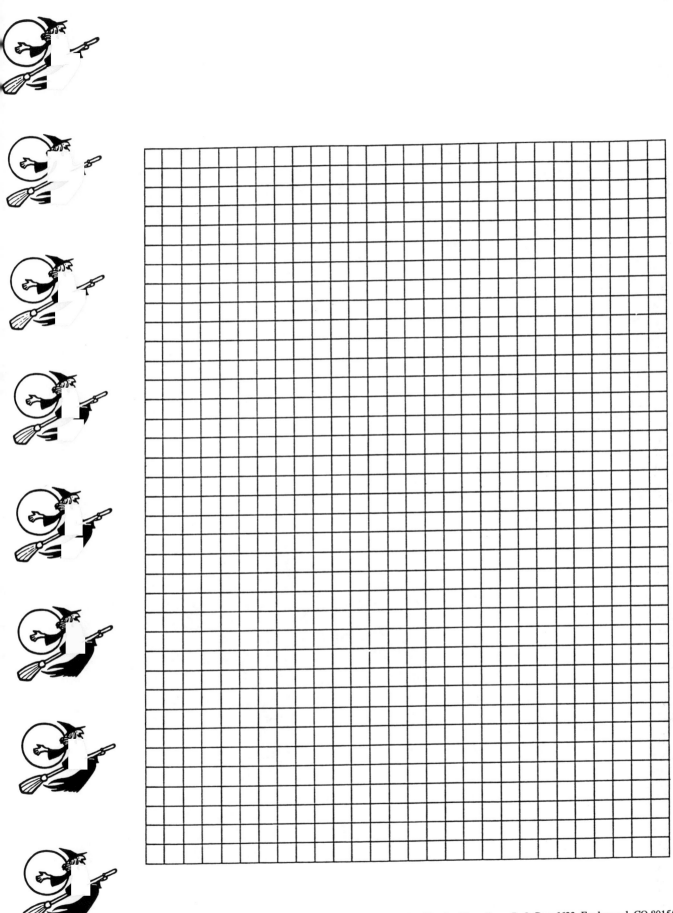

From Pumpkin Time to Valentines. Copyright 1994. Susan Ohanian. Teacher Ideas Press, P. O. Box 6633, Englewood, CO 80155.

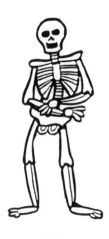

Ghoulish Grass

Read About It

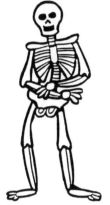

Some plants have names that would make an interesting ghoul garden if you drew them to look like their names. For example: what would a garden of hogweed, elephant grass, dogwood, horseradish, and cow parsley look like? Check a gardening book for other names of zany-sounding plants to fill this garden. Then, draw your garden!

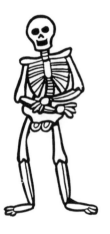

From Pumpkin Time to Valentines. Copyright 1994. Susan Ohanian. Teacher Ideas Press, P. O. Box 6633, Englewood, CO 80155.

A Cartoonist's Halloween

Think About It

If you were drawing a cartoon called *California* or *Hawaii Witch*, you might draw a witch standing up on her broomstick as though it were a surfboard.

Draw It

Draw a cartoon titled *Texas Witch*, *Colorado Witch*, *Vermont Witch*, *Florida Witch*, *Georgia Witch*, or any other geographic witch you can think of.

A Thumbnail Sketch

Think About It

Make a Halloween picture by decorating your thumbprint. If you want some ideas, check out Ed Emberley's *Great Thumbprint Drawing Book*.

Thumb pumpkin   Thumb bat

Now it's your turn:

From Pumpkin Time to Valentines. Copyright 1994. Susan Ohanian. Teacher Ideas Press, P. O. Box 6633, Englewood, CO 80155.

Change It

Read About It

Familiar Mother Goose rhymes can be turned into Halloween rhymes. Here's a sample:

Mary Had a Little Bat

Mary had a little bat
Its wings as black as night.
Everywhere that Mary went
That bat also took flight.
It followed her to school one day
Which was against the rules.
It made the children shriek and cry
To see a bat at school.

Write About It

Now it's your turn. Turn your favorite Mother Goose rhyme into a Halloween rhyme. You might try *Old Mother Hubbard, Little Jack Horner,* or *Jack and Jill.*

From Pumpkin Time to Valentines. Copyright 1994. Susan Ohanian. Teacher Ideas Press, P. O. Box 6633, Englewood, CO 80155.

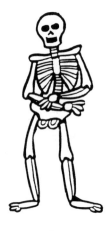

A Moving Message

Think About It

Make a hidden-message-under-the-flap Halloween card to send from one literary character to another.

> Example: Little Red Riding Hood might write to the Wolf: "Have a great Howl-o-ween."

What might the wolf write back?

You can use these directions to design the card the wolf will send, or adapt the directions for any other fairy tale character.

1. Cut two pieces of paper the same size. One is for the pop-up wolf head. The other is the outside of the card. Fold the sheet for the wolf's head in half. Cut on the solid line. Fold on the dotted line.

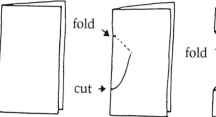

2. Open the paper and push the pop-up up inside the card. Refold the card with the pop-up on the inside.

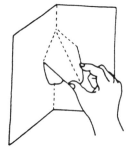

3. Close the card with the pop-up inside and press the folds.

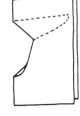

4. Open the card. The pop-up is the wolf's snout. Draw the rest of the wolf's face.

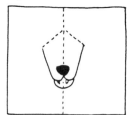
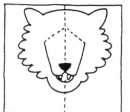
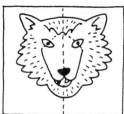

5. Fold the outside sheet in half and paste the pop-up inside it. Close the card and press the center fold. Open it and write your message.

(Adapted from *Within the Forest* by Susan Ohanian.)

From Pumpkin Time to Valentines. Copyright 1994. Susan Ohanian. Teacher Ideas Press, P. O. Box 6633, Englewood, CO 80155.

UNICEF

Read About It

In ancient times people celebrated All Hallows Eve by baking cakes to give to the poor. In modern times children collect money for UNICEF. UNICEF was founded in 1946 to give food, clothing, and blankets to children who needed help at the end of World War II. The letters stand for United Nations International Children's Emergency Fund. Children around the world still need food and medicine and "Trick or Treat for UNICEF" brings them that help.

"Trick or Treat for UNICEF" began in 1950 when a Philadelphia youth group, concerned over the plight of the world's children, took up a door-to-door collection using empty milk cartons. They raised $17. Since then, American children have raised over one million dollars for UNICEF. Some of their projects have included:

√ Walk-a-thon or Trick-or-Treat Trot: Collect pledges for each half-mile you walk or run.

√ Skip-a-Snack: Donate the money saved on a snack or a meal and gain greater awareness of world hunger.

√ Read-a-Thon: Select books from authors around the world and collect a pledge for each book you finish.

√ Recycling Drive: Clean up your community environment and donate the money raised to help the world's children.

If you and your classmates want to know how to participate in this modern Halloween tradition, your class can obtain a curriculum guide and "Trick-or-Treat for UNICEF" materials by contacting:

The U. S. Committee for UNICEF
P.O. Box 182248
Chattanooga, TN 37422-7248

Research It

Find out more about what UNICEF does for needy children around the world.

Draw It

Make a poster about UNICEF to display in your classroom or somewhere else in the school.

From Pumpkin Time to Valentines. Copyright 1994. Susan Ohanian. Teacher Ideas Press, P. O. Box 6633, Englewood, CO 80155.

Celebrate February:
Friendship Month

Valentine's Day

People aren't sure about the true story of how Valentine's celebrations got started. There are eight Saint Valentines in the Catholic church's official records on saints and several Valentine legends.

According to one version of the story a Roman priest named Valentine was beaten, stoned, and beheaded on February 14, 269 C.E. because he defied the order of Emperor Claudius II to stop performing marriages. Claudius II had canceled all marriage ceremonies because he was engaged in a war with the invading Goths and he was having trouble finding enough soldiers for his army.

According to another version, one you can read about in *Saint Valentine* by Robert Sabuda, Valentine was a humble physician in ancient Rome. A religious man, Valentine took the dangerous step of becoming a Christian, praying to just one god rather than many Roman gods. He prayed for his patients, including the blind daughter of a jailer. When Valentine was thrown into jail along with other Christians, he gave the jailer a message written on a small scroll of papyrus. "Give this to your daughter," he said. When the blind child took the scroll a crocus fell from it. Her father read the message, "from your Valentine" and magically the girl could see. Valentine was executed on February 14, 270 C.E. in a persecution of Christians. According to legend, Pope Julius I built a basilica over Valentine's grave, and in 496 C.E. Pope Gelasius I named February 14 as Saint Valentine's Day.

Another version of this tale has Valentine falling in love with his jailer's blind daughter and curing her with love letters from prison signed "from your Valentine."

Another Roman tradition, the feast of Lupercalia, is also connected with Valentine's Day. Lupercus, one of many Roman gods, was the god of animals, forests, and shepherds. A feast in his honor was held on February 15. One of the customs was for unmarried women to write love messages and put them in a large urn. An unmarried man would pick a message and become the message writer's partner for the rest of the festival. They would promise to remain friends for the new year (which began in March). Lynda Graham-Barber, author of *Mushy! The Complete Book of Valentine Words*, suggests that this ancient Roman urn may have been the very first valentine box.

From Pumpkin Time to Valentines. Copyright 1994. Susan Ohanian. Teacher Ideas Press, P. O. Box 6633, Englewood, CO 80155.

Graham-Barber also has an interesting note on the origin of the word *Lupercalia*. She says it means "festival of the wolf" and points out that according to popular legend a female wolf nursed the twins Romulus and Remus, the founders of Rome. The Romans believed wolves possessed strong sexual power. Think about the meaning of calling a man a "wolf," or the term "wolf whistle."

Another source for the origins of Valentine's Day comes from medieval lore. People then believed that birds claimed their mates on February 14. So people of that time linked the death of St. Valentine and bird mating with human courtship and love.

People linked birds to their own lives. According to superstition, if a woman saw a robin on Valentine's Day, she'd marry a sailor; if she saw a sparrow she'd marry a poor man and be happy; and if she saw a goldfinch she'd marry a millionaire.

A medieval practice in England was for unmarried women to write their names on pieces of paper and put them in a bowl. An unmarried man would take a name and pin it on his sleeve. (Did you ever hear the expression "to wear your heart on your sleeve"?) He also gave her small gifts and promised to protect her in the new year.

From Pumpkin Time to Valentines. Copyright 1994. Susan Ohanian. Teacher Ideas Press, P. O. Box 6633, Englewood, CO 80155.

Big and Little

Read About It

Ruth Krauss writes about big and little things that go together:

> Big forests
> love
> little trees.
> Big fields
> love
> little flowers.
> Big monkeys
> love
> little monkeyshines
> and I love you.

Write About It

Think of your own big and little things that go together.

Big_____

love

little_____.

Big_____

love

little_____.

and I love you.

From Pumpkin Time to Valentines. Copyright 1994. Susan Ohanian. Teacher Ideas Press, P. O. Box 6633, Englewood, CO 80155.

I Love You, I Love You

Read About It

Here is a famous chant. Notice that the last line has a surprise. Is the speaker of this verse offering much?

> I love you, I love you,
> I love you so well;
> If I had a peanut,
> I'd give you the shell.

Write About It

Use this pattern to make up your own surprise chant. You will notice that in the chant, the third and last lines rhyme. A thesaurus and a rhyming dictionary will help you find a rhyme for your own chant.

Hint: You might find it easier to write the third and fourth lines before you write the second line.

> I love you, I love you,
>
> I love you so _____;
>
> If I had a _____,
>
> I'd give you the _____.

Extra Credit

Once you have your chant, you may want to turn it into a greeting card. Try making a moveable card: a flap card or pop-up card.

From Pumpkin Time to Valentines. Copyright 1994. Susan Ohanian. Teacher Ideas Press, P. O. Box 6633, Englewood, CO 80155.

My Love Is Like . . .

Read About It

This is an old English valentine rhyme.

My Love Is Like a Cabbage

My love is like a cabbage
   Divided into two,
The leaves I give to others
   But the heart I give to you.

Think About It

Come up with your own *My love is like . . .* rhyme. (Hint: can you think of other fruits, vegetables, and flowers that have hearts? If something doesn't have a heart, you can substitute *core*.)

Here's another example:

My love is like a watermelon
   Divided in two,
The rind I give to others
   But the core I give to you.

Write About It

Now it's your turn. Write your own rhyme. Then turn it into a card. Give it to someone who makes your school a better place to be.

1. My love is like a . . .

2. My love is like a . . .

3. My love is like a . . .

From Pumpkin Time to Valentines. Copyright 1994. Susan Ohanian. Teacher Ideas Press, P. O. Box 6633, Englewood, CO 80155.

I Love You More Than . . .

Read About It

I Love You More than Applesauce
Jack Prelutsky

I love you more than applesauce,
than peaches and a plum,
than chocolate hearts and cherry tarts
and berry bubblegum.
I love you more than lemonade
and seven-layer cakes,
than lollipops and candy drops
and thick vanilla shakes.

(From *It's Valentine's Day* by Jack Prelutsky.)

Write About It

Make a list of at least 25 things you like a lot. You can list food, toys, games, songs, and anything else you like. Next, check to see if any of the items on your list rhyme. If they don't, try coming up with more words that do rhyme (even if you don't like them a lot). For help, reread Jack Prelutsky's poem and notice which of his words rhyme.

Then write your own *I love you more than . . .* poem.

From Pumpkin Time to Valentines. Copyright 1994. Susan Ohanian. Teacher Ideas Press, P. O. Box 6633, Englewood, CO 80155.

I Love You More . . . Again

Write About It

Try the pattern in Jack Prelutsky's poem in the voice of different people. You can use some of the suggestions below or get together with three buddy writers and make a list of other possible voices.

A truck driver might say:
>   I love you more than eighteen-wheelers,
>   than CBs and a horn.

A teacher might say:
>   I love you more than erasers,
>   than chalkboards and a desk.

Now it's your turn. Try the *I love you more than . . .* pattern in several voices. You may use these or come up with some others.

Musician
Athlete
Clown
Carpenter
Clockmaker
Fireman
Pilot
Zookeeper
Jockey
Waitress
Dog groomer
Hair stylist
Chef

From Pumpkin Time to Valentines. Copyright 1994. Susan Ohanian. Teacher Ideas Press, P. O. Box 6633, Englewood, CO 80155.

A Very Merry Valentine Card

Read About It

Read this valentine message and see if you notice anything special about the words.

> Very merry Valentine's to you,
> Each and every one.
> Rejoice. Applaud. Laugh. Please do.
> You must get ready for some fun.
> Make merry. Tell a joke today.
> Everyone laughing and reading rhymes,
> Rooms full of cards and sweets and play,
> Rooms where it is sunshine time.
> Yes, have a very fine
> Valentine's:
> Amusing
> Loving
> Entertaining
> Nifty
> Terrific
> Intriguing
> Noteworthy
> Excellent
> Stupendous.

Write About It

Your turn! Choose your own valentine phrase, such as "Very Merry Valentine's," for example. Write the phrase vertically on your paper. Then turn it into a poem by writing a word or short phrase beginning with each letter.

From Pumpkin Time to Valentines. Copyright 1994. Susan Ohanian. Teacher Ideas Press, P. O. Box 6633, Englewood, CO 80155.

Tongue Twisters

Read About It

See if you can read these famous tongue twisters three times each out loud to a buddy reader. Read them as fast as you can.

Toy boat, toy boat, toy boat

A big baby buggy with rubber buggy bumpers.

Black bug's blood, black bug's blood.

She sells sea shells by the seashore.

Peter Piper picked a peck of pickled peppers,
a peck of pickled peppers Peter Piper picked.
But if Peter Piper picked a peck of pickled peppers,
where is the peck of pickled peppers Peter Piper picked?

Write About It

Your turn. Write a valentine tongue twister with your buddy reader. Then see if anybody in your class can read it out loud.

From Pumpkin Time to Valentines. Copyright 1994. Susan Ohanian. Teacher Ideas Press, P. O. Box 6633, Englewood, CO 80155.

Favorite Red Things

| Talk About It |

Interview three people—adults and children. Ask them to tell you about their favorite red things. When you have finished the interviews, compare your results with what your classmates found. Make a graph of the ten most popular red choices your class discovered.

Interviewee 1 _____

Here are my favorite red things:

1.

2.

3.

Interviewee 2 _____

Here are my favorite red things:

1.

2.

3.

Interviewee 3 _____

Here are my favorite red things:

1.

2.

3.

From Pumpkin Time to Valentines. Copyright 1994. Susan Ohanian. Teacher Ideas Press, P. O. Box 6633, Englewood, CO 80155.

Talk to a Friend

| Talk About It |

Since February is the month for fun with friends, interview a friend. Before you start your interview, write down at least three questions: things you'd like to find out about your friend. As you are talking with your friend, try to come up with more questions, but make sure you have at least three to start with.

1.

2.

3.

4.

5.

6.

From Pumpkin Time to Valentines. Copyright 1994. Susan Ohanian. Teacher Ideas Press, P. O. Box 6633, Englewood, CO 80155.

How Did They Meet?

Read About It

David Macaulay (author-illustrator of *Cathedral, City, Pyramid,* and *The Way Things Work*) first wrote letters to, then met the woman who later became his wife. He was writing books in the United States. She was his editor and lived in England.

Talk About It

Interview some adults you know. Find out how they met their spouse or a very good friend.

Interviewee 1 _____

Interviewee 2 _____

Interviewee 3 _____

From Pumpkin Time to Valentines. Copyright 1994. Susan Ohanian. Teacher Ideas Press, P. O. Box 6633, Englewood, CO 80155.

Getting to Know You

Read About It

Because of Lozo Brown, by Larry King, *Chester's Way* by Kevin Henkes, and *Crusher Is Coming* by Bob Graham are stories about children who discover new things about other children they think they know—or think they don't want to know.

The narrator of *Because of Lozo Brown* describes the new boy who has moved next door:

> He hasn't said a word to me
> But I can tell he's mean.
> I bet his breath is terrible.
> I bet his tongue is green.
> I bet big rats live in his hair
> and he roars and growls like a grizzly bear.

Talk About It

Since February is the month for friendship, find out more about someone you don't know very well. Interview this person, and make a new friend!

Before you start your interview, write down at least two questions. As you are talking with your new friend, you should think of at least three more questions.

1.

2.

3.

4.

5.

What's one thing you and your new friend agree about?

From Pumpkin Time to Valentines. Copyright 1994. Susan Ohanian. Teacher Ideas Press, P. O. Box 6633, Englewood, CO 80155.

What Would *You* Do?

Read About It

In *213 Valentines* by Barbara Cohen, Wade Thompson changes schools. Missing his old school and his old friends, he is convinced that people at his new school are snobs and that nobody will send him any valentines.

So he figures a way to solve the problem—he spends $32.33 buying valentines to send to himself. He soon runs out of phrases such as *Your Secret Admirer, Your Friend,* and *Won't You Be Mine,* and he starts signing his valentine's cards: Patrick Ewing, Michael Jordan, Bo Jackson, Jackie Robinson, Muhammed Ali, Willie Mays, Joe Louis, Arthur Ashe, Aretha Franklin, Prince, Eddie Murphy, Bill Cosby, George Washington Carver, Jesse Jackson, Oprah Winfrey, Martin Luther King, and so on. Even then, he runs out of names so he looks in the phone book and copies out names he likes the look of: Charles Retajczyk, Eugenia Flagtown, Samuel Brescakin, Malastesta Mazzocchinni, Irwin Chocolate, and so on.

Write About It

Make a list of some famous or fictional people you'd like to receive a valentine from. These people can be names in the news, names from history, or interesting-sounding names out of the phone book.

Talk About It

Read your list to at least two friends. Listen to their lists.

Do you have any names in common?
Which names on their lists surprised you? Why?
Which names on your list surprised them?
Make yourself a card with a message from someone on your list.

From Pumpkin Time to Valentines. Copyright 1994. Susan Ohanian. Teacher Ideas Press, P. O. Box 6633, Englewood, CO 80155.

Count the Ways to Make a Friend

Talk About It

Talk to two or three classmates about how you might help someone who has just moved to a new school. Make a list of suggestions for making new friends.

Write About It

Make a poster listing friendship tips.

From Pumpkin Time to Valentines. Copyright 1994. Susan Ohanian. Teacher Ideas Press, P. O. Box 6633, Englewood, CO 80155.

A Silly Valentine

Read About It

In *A Valentine for Ms. Vanilla* by Fred Ehrlich, the children have fun writing some offbeat valentine's messages to each other. Here are some other silly valentine's messages.

> Valentine, I'll be yours,
> Even when it rains or pours.
>
> If you'll be my Valentine today,
> I won't take your books away.
>
> I'll be your Valentine, I guess,
> Just stop calling me a pest.

Write About It

Now it's your turn. Write a few off-beat valentine rhymes of your own. Notice in the samples that the humor is helped by the fact that one of the rhyming words is positive and the other negative. Here are some positive-negative pairs to help you get started. Think of at least three more pairs before you write your own silly rhymes.

dirt/flirt	bug/hug	squirrel/pearl;	flu/true
waste/haste	snake/break	whine/mine	

From Pumpkin Time to Valentines. Copyright 1994. Susan Ohanian. Teacher Ideas Press, P. O. Box 6633, Englewood, CO 80155.

Roses Are Red . . .

Read About It

We all know that familiar Valentine rhyme:

> Roses are red,
> Violets are blue,
> Sugar is sweet,
> And so are you.

Read these flower names aloud with at least one other buddy reader. Enjoy the names. Then try to come up with a valentine rhyme for some of them. You may want to do some research in the library for plant information. Or you may choose a plant just because you like its name.

Bleeding heart

Daisy

Dragon plant

Petunia

Hen and chickens

Reindeer moss

Fishbone plant

Honeysuckle

Morning glory

Cattail

Buttercup

Crow toe

Dandelion

Dogwood

Forget-me-not

Elephant-ear fern

Johnny-jump-up

Mouse-ear

Canary grass

Spiderflower

Tiger jaw

Venus-flytrap

Bachelor's button

Spider lily

Bluebonnet

Candytuft

Cherokee Rose

Chinese houses

Skunkweed

Cup-and-saucer

Devil's-tongue

Turtlehead

Dutchman's-pipe

Indian blanket

Liverleaf

Queen Anne's lace

From Pumpkin Time to Valentines. Copyright 1994. Susan Ohanian. Teacher Ideas Press, P. O. Box 6633, Englewood, CO 80155.

Animal Puns

Read About It

Sometimes the sound of an animal's name can be turned into a funny valentine message. For example, "Iguana be yours!" or "Snake, rattle and roll into my heart."

I'm Beary Happy To Be Your Valentine.

You Otter Be Mine.

Write About It

Try coming up with a funny valentine expression to go with some creatures. Then make a Creature Card and give it to someone who makes your school a better place to be.

Be My Valentinosaur.

From Pumpkin Time to Valentines. Copyright 1994. Susan Ohanian. Teacher Ideas Press, P. O. Box 6633, Englewood, CO 80155.

You're Dog-Gone Terrific!

Think About It

Sometimes the characteristics of an animal can be turned into a funny Valentine message. For example, *You're DOG-gone terrific!* and *You're the PURRfect pal.*

Be TOADally Mine.

I Don't Give a Hoot
For Anyone But You.

Write About It

Design a card with one of the DOG-gone terrific ideas on this page, or come up with your PURRfect animal valentine on your own.

Don't be a slowpoke.
I'll raise a stink if you aren't mine.
Stop horsing around.
Hoppy Valentine's Day!
I don't give a hoot for anyone but you.
Be cool. Be mine.
You're a good egg, Valentine.
Don't be a bird brain. Be my Valentine.
Come out of your shell.

Be Cool.
Be Mine.

From Pumpkin Time to Valentines. Copyright 1994. Susan Ohanian. Teacher Ideas Press, P. O. Box 6633, Englewood, CO 80155.

Animal Idioms

Write About It

Create a valentine that uses one of these animal expressions, which are called idioms:

A fine kettle of fish	Bats in the belfry
Stop horsing around	Take the bull by the horns
Let's talk turkey	A whale of a time
Birds of a feather	Busy as a bee
Teach an old dog new tricks	The cat's meow
The cat that swallowed the canary	For the birds
Hogwash	Let the cat out of the hat
A little bird told me	Memory like an elephant
Monkey see, monkey do	A snake in the grass
Stir up a hornet's nest	Stubborn as a mule
To lead a dog's life	A rat race
Barking up the wrong tree	Wise as an owl
A bee in your bonnet	Go hog wild

From Pumpkin Time to Valentines. Copyright 1994. Susan Ohanian. Teacher Ideas Press, P. O. Box 6633, Englewood, CO 80155.

I'm TOADally Yours

Look at It

When a frog is in love it sends a special message:

"I love your big bulging eyes and your wet green skin."

Write and Draw About It

Create your own animal valentine cartoon. Be sure to include special characteristics of the animal you have chosen. For example, if you write a wolf valentine, you might mention the type of teeth it has. What might a hippopotamus compliment be? A ladybug? A turtle?

You may want to go to the library to check out some animal facts and faces. You can look in an encyclopedia or in a nonfiction book about an animal that interests you. The Eyewitness series (Knopf) and Caroline Arnold's animal series (Morrow) have lots of interesting titles and fascinating facts.

From Pumpkin Time to Valentines. Copyright 1994. Susan Ohanian. Teacher Ideas Press, P. O. Box 6633, Englewood, CO 80155.

I Love Your Wet, Slimy Skin

Read About It

In *Charles and Claudine* by Harold Berson, we read this description of a frog named Claudine:

> Claudine, with her exquisite green-spotted brown skin, her delicate feet, and her golden eyes was stunning.

Maybe it takes another frog to see a frog's skin as exquisite but you can make anything sound good or bad by the words you choose to describe it. For example, you can call a car a *limousine* or an *old clunker*. On the chart below, write positive and negative descriptions for as many animals as you can.

ANIMAL	POSITIVE	NEGATIVE
Frog	dew-drop moist skin	wet, slimy skin

From Pumpkin Time to Valentines. Copyright 1994. Susan Ohanian. Teacher Ideas Press, P. O. Box 6633, Englewood, CO 80155.

I Love You to the Core

Directions: Take a look at these foods and see if you can come up with a funny valentine message for each one.

You are the apple of my eye, Valentine.

I'm in the pits if you won't be mine.

Be a good egg and be my Valentine.

I'm as cool as a cucumber when you're my Valentine.

I'll eat my hat if you aren't my Valentine.

I'm in a pickle until you are my Valentine.

From Pumpkin Time to Valentines. Copyright 1994. Susan Ohanian. Teacher Ideas Press, P. O. Box 6633, Englewood, CO 80155.

You Stand the Test of Time, Valentine

Looking Closely

An expression such as "You stand the test of time," takes on a different meaning when you see it on an ancient Egyptian mummy. Can you think of another illustration that would fit with the phrase "You stand the test of time, Valentine"?

Draw It

Try illustrating one or more of these expressions:

I'm sitting on top of the world when you're mine.

You swept me off my feet.

Rise to the occasion and be my Valentine.

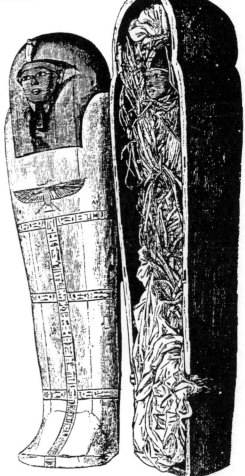

From Pumpkin Time to Valentines. Copyright 1994. Susan Ohanian. Teacher Ideas Press, P. O. Box 6633, Englewood, CO 80155.

Valentines in History

Read About It

You can create a funny historical valentine by finding an idiom that uses words connected to something in a famous person's life.

First match each of these idioms with a historic figure. For example:

Paul Revere's wife might send him a valentine that said,
Stop horsing around and be my Valentine!

Try matching these idioms with famous figures who could use them in a funny valentine.

1. I'll take you for a ride.
2. I'll light up your life.
3. You're the apple of my eye.
4. I'm just letting off steam.
5. Let your hair down.

6. Go fly a kite!
7. We're birds of a feather.
8. Face the music.
9. Let the chips fall where they may.
10. I can paddle my own canoe.

a) Elvis Presley
b) Thomas Edison
c) Henry Ford
d) Benjamin Franklin
e) Robert Fulton

f) John Chapman
g) Big Bird
h) Sacagawea
i) president of a chocolate company
j) Rapunzel

Now that you have your matches, create valentines for at least three of these figures. It can be a valentine they would send or receive.

Extra Challenge

Create or find an idiom that matches up with a different famous figure.

From Pumpkin Time to Valentines. Copyright 1994. Susan Ohanian. Teacher Ideas Press, P. O. Box 6633, Englewood, CO 80155.

Valentines for the Famous

Thinker's Challenge

What people in the news (past or present) might say the following in a valentine message?

1. Don't cry over spilled milk.
2. Cold feet
3. A cold shoulder
4. To land on one's feet
5. To blow the whistle on someone.

6. Bury the hatchet
7. To work like clockwork
8. Climbing the walls
9. All washed up
10. Bite the bullet

SHARE your answers with at least two friends.

Make at least two valentines using your ideas. Create a *Valentines for the Famous* bulletin board.

From Pumpkin Time to Valentines. Copyright 1994. Susan Ohanian. Teacher Ideas Press, P. O. Box 6633, Englewood, CO 80155.

Have a Heart

Write and Draw About It

Here are some heart-y expressions. Use as many as you want to create some funny valentines.

heartstrings
heartburn
heart of gold
learn by heart
"Deep in the Heart of Texas"
have a heart
heart of the matter
heart in one's mouth
take heart
chicken-hearted
down-hearted
half-hearted
heart-to-heart talk
heart of stone
broken hearted
eat your heart out
a hard heart
to lose heart
to make one's heart leap
to wear one's heart on one's sleeve
my heart sank

From Pumpkin Time to Valentines. Copyright 1994. Susan Ohanian. Teacher Ideas Press, P. O. Box 6633, Englewood, CO 80155.

How Do I Love Thee?

Read About It

People with different occupations might answer the question "How do I love thee?" in different ways. Look at these examples:

Cardiologist: with all my heart
Clockmaker: for all time
Optician: It was love at first sight.

Write About It

Now come up with some valentine answers to the question "How do I love thee?" for these occupations.

travel agent:

astronaut:

football player:

teacher:

newscaster:

truck driver:

veterinarian:

mathematician:

grocer:

governor:

artist:

musician:

Extra Challenge

Now create your own occupational valentines.

From Pumpkin Time to Valentines. Copyright 1994. Susan Ohanian. Teacher Ideas Press, P. O. Box 6633, Englewood, CO 80155.

Valentine Pairs

Read About It

Here are some famous pairs in literature:

Max and the Wild Things
Frog and Toad
Winnie the Pooh and Christopher Robin
Goldilocks and the Three Bears
Little Red Riding Hood and the Wolf
Paul Bunyan and Babe, the Blue Ox
Lois Lane and Superman
Sherlock Holmes and Watson

Think About It

Come up with some other literary pairs. This is a good activity to do in pairs. Find a partner to work with you.

1.

2.

3.

Write About It

Create a valentine for one of these pairs. Have one part of the pair send a valentine to the other.

From Pumpkin Time to Valentines. Copyright 1994. Susan Ohanian. Teacher Ideas Press, P. O. Box 6633, Englewood, CO 80155.

More Valentine Pairs

Read About It

Here are some famous pairs in history. Some are married; others are paired because of similar accomplishments. You may want to work with a partner to learn about these pairs.

George and Martha Washington

John and Abigail Adams

Amelia Earhart and Charles Lindbergh

John Glenn and Sally Ride

Magic Johnson and Larry Bird

Write About It

List as many famous pairs as you can. They can be from history, television, sports, music, movies, or anywhere else you think of.

Create a valentine one of these pairs might send to the other.

From Pumpkin Time to Valentines. Copyright 1994. Susan Ohanian. Teacher Ideas Press, P. O. Box 6633, Englewood, CO 80155.

Things That Go Together

Read About It

Charlotte Zolotow wrote a book called *Some Things Go Together*. Here is a sample of her pairs:

> Peace with dove
> Home with love
> Gardens with flowers
> Clocks with hours
> Sky with blue,
> And me with you.

Here's one more sample—this one from a third grade class:

> Pen with ink;
> Skate with rink.
> Pizza with cheese;
> Will you please
> BE MY VALENTINE.

Write About It

Now it's your turn. Since this is about pairs, you may want to find a buddy to work with you. Make a list of at least ten pairs of things that go together. Then see if you can turn your list into rhyming pairs for a special valentine message for someone you care about.

From Pumpkin Time to Valentines. Copyright 1994. Susan Ohanian. Teacher Ideas Press, P. O. Box 6633, Englewood, CO 80155.

Valentine Garden

Read About It

In the nineteenth century, picture puzzle valentines called rebuses were very popular. Try to solve this one.

Rebus Valentine

You may not  all for me

The way I care for you.

You may  your nose

when I plead with you—

But if your should with mine

Forever hope

There is no reason in the world

Why we two !

Write About It

Now it's your turn. Write a valentine rebus message using these foods (and any others you can think of):
orange (hint: orange you glad it's Valentine's Day?)

beet	onion
berry	peas
grapes	honeydew melon
cabbage	_____

From Pumpkin Time to Valentines. Copyright 1994. Susan Ohanian. Teacher Ideas Press, P. O. Box 6633, Englewood, CO 80155.

Solve the Message

Read About It

Look at how these pictures and numbers help send a valentine message.

My ♥ 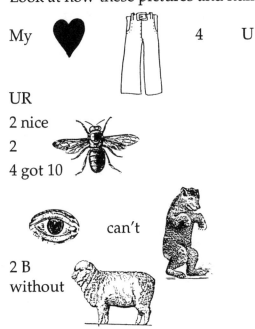   4   U

UR
2 nice
2
4 got 10

Challenge

Once you've solved the messages above, create one of your own.

From Pumpkin Time to Valentines. Copyright 1994. Susan Ohanian. Teacher Ideas Press, P. O. Box 6633, Englewood, CO 80155.

Hard Hearts

Figure It Out

Look at these boxes very carefully. Each box contains a hidden valentine message (in capital letters). It is a familiar saying, or idiom. These messages are tricky . . . very tricky!

Be sure to study the way the letters and words are placed in each box. The first one is solved for you. Notice that you had to come up with synonyms to find the familiar idiom. Have fun!

```
I'M

PACING
ATMOSPHERE

When You're My Valentine
```

I'm walking on air

When you're my Valentine

```
I'M

POSING
EARTH

When You're My Valentine
```

```
Be My Valentine

EVER               EVER
EVER
EVER
EVER
```

```
I'M MYSELF

If You Aren't My Valentine
```

From Pumpkin Time to Valentines. Copyright 1994. Susan Ohanian. Teacher Ideas Press, P. O. Box 6633, Englewood, CO 80155.

More Hard Hearts

Think About It

Follow the directions from *Hard Hearts* to figure out these puzzles. Good luck!
These are tricky. . .very tricky!

DON'T   THINK
              THINK

Be My Valentine

EARS EARS EARS EARS
EARS EARS EARS EARS
EARS EARS EARS EARS
EARS EARS EARS EARS

    Waiting to Hear
    You're My Valentine

DRY

unless you're my Valentine

SMART   BRIGHT
INTELLIGENT   CLEVER

Don't Be Ignorant.
Be My Valentine.

From Pumpkin Time to Valentines. Copyright 1994. Susan Ohanian. Teacher Ideas Press, P. O. Box 6633, Englewood, CO 80155.

Celebrating American Heart Month

Read About It

Research the heart. Write down at least three interesting things you discover about the heart.

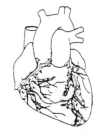

Fascinating Heart Fact 1.

Fascinating Heart Fact 2.

Fascinating Heart Fact 3.

Fascinating Heart Fact 4.

From Pumpkin Time to Valentines. Copyright 1994. Susan Ohanian. Teacher Ideas Press, P. O. Box 6633, Englewood, CO 80155.

Heartbeats

Find Out

1. How many times does your heart beat a minute?

2. How many times does it beat in a day? a year?

3. How does exercise affect your heartbeat?

Challenge

Find Out: Do some research and find out the heartbeats per minute of the following creatures:

whale	
elephant	
bird	
mouse	
insect	

From Pumpkin Time to Valentines. Copyright 1994. Susan Ohanian. Teacher Ideas Press, P. O. Box 6633, Englewood, CO 80155.

Ninety-nine Valentines on the Wall . . .

Read About It

Look at Ian Serraillier's number rhyme in his poem:

Going Steady

Valentine, O Valentine
I'll be your love and you'll be mine:
We'll care for each other, rain or fine,
And in ninety years we'll be ninety-nine.

(In *Valentine Poems*, Myra Cohn Livingston.)

Think About It

How many numbers can you find rhymes for? Make a list.

One	Thirteen
Two	Twenty
Three	Thirty
Four	Forty
Five	Fifty
Six	Sixty
Seven	Seventy
Eight	Eighty
Nine	Ninety
Ten	Hundred
Eleven	Thousand
Twelve	Million

Challenge

Can you turn any of your number rhymes into a valentine poem?

From Pumpkin Time to Valentines. Copyright 1994. Susan Ohanian. Teacher Ideas Press, P. O. Box 6633, Englewood, CO 80155.

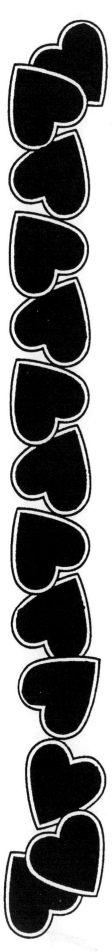

328 Friends

Read About It

In Marjorie Weinman Sharmat's *The 329th Friend* Emery Raccoon invites 328 strangers to lunch in the hope that at least one will want to be his friend:

> Emery's guests arrived one by one and in pairs, three, fours, fives, tens, twenties, and fifties.

Think About It

If you were in charge of games for this party, how many different teams could you have? (You get to decide how many people are on a team.)

Think Some More
Emery says "Hello. Glad to see you." 328 times as he greets his guests. How long do you think it would take a person to say that 328 times? Make a prediction with a buddy and then time each other. You may discover that you need two buddies for this: one to time you and one to count.

More Problems
How many dishes and how much silverware would you need for a party of this size?

Find a recipe for good party food. Notice how many it serves. Rewrite it to serve you and 328 friends.

From Pumpkin Time to Valentines. Copyright 1994. Susan Ohanian. Teacher Ideas Press, P. O. Box 6633, Englewood, CO 80155.

By the Numbers

| Read About It |

You can astound your friends and family with this valentine number trick. Show them five paper hearts, each covered with numbers. Ask a friend to think of a number between 1 and 31, and point to the hearts with that number. Then you "read your friend's mind" by guessing the number.

The Trick

1. Cut out these five hearts.

2. The number at the bottom point of each heart is your key (1, 2, 4, 8, and 16).

3. As your friend points to the hearts that contain the number he or she selected, add those key numbers. For example, if your friend chooses the number 21, he would point to the hearts with the key numbers 1, 4, and 16, which add up to 21.

This activity is adapted from *Valentine Magic* by James Baker. The book also gives a more boggling version of this trick, as well as other tricks.

From Pumpkin Time to Valentines. Copyright 1994. Susan Ohanian. Teacher Ideas Press, P. O. Box 6633, Englewood, CO 80155.

With a Song in My Heart

Listen to This

Here are a few gold records about the heart. These records each sold at least a million copies. Do you know any of the songs? Ask your parents and other adults if they know any of the words. You can also ask a librarian for resources you can check for song lyrics.

1956 "Heartbreak Hotel," Elvis Presley

1957 "That's When Your Heartache Begins," Elvis Presley

1963 "I Left My Heart in San Francisco," Tony Bennett

1967 "Sergeant Pepper's Lonely Hearts Club Band," The Beatles

1969 "Your Cheatin' Heart," Hank Williams

Do you know any songs about the heart?
How about songs of love?
Write down the words.

From Pumpkin Time to Valentines. Copyright 1994. Susan Ohanian. Teacher Ideas Press, P. O. Box 6633, Englewood, CO 80155.

I Love You In London

Read About It

In *Arthur's Valentine* by Marc Brown, Arthur has a mystery. Someone is sending him secret valentine messages. Here's one he received:

> I love you in London,
> I love you in Rome,
> Look in your mailbox
> When you get home.
> XOXOXOXOXOXOXOXOXOX
> Your Secret Admirer

Write About It

Put on your geography thinking cap. Create your own place name valentine. To get started, write down the names of 10 cities and states in the United States and Canada. Then write down 10 foreign cities and countries. Next, look for rhymes and choose the ones you will use for your valentine verse.
HINT: If you get stuck, check out an atlas.

You can follow Marc Brown's pattern if you want:

I love you in _____

I love you in _____

_____

_____.

Helpful Hint: Mark the lines that need to rhyme.
Alternative: You can make up your own pattern.

From Pumpkin Time to Valentines. Copyright 1994. Susan Ohanian. Teacher Ideas Press, P. O. Box 6633, Englewood, CO 80155.

On Top of Heart Mountain

Read About It

For this project you need a large piece of paper. Your first job is to draw a large outline map of the United States or Canada. You may want to team up with other students to draw this map. Your map needs to show the state boundary lines.

When you have made your map, check out some atlases. See if you can find a valentine-related word for each state. Here are a few real place names to help you get started. You can find out where they are located:

Heart Mountain

Sweetwater

Sweethome

Loveland

Kissimee

Romance

Multicultural Ways to Be a Friend

Read About It

Read how to say *heart* in many languages:

Arabic:	qalb
Czech:	srdce
Danish:	hjerte
Dutch:	hart
French:	coeur
German:	herz
Greek:	kardia
Hebrew:	lev
Hungarian:	sziv
Italian:	cuore
Polish:	serce
Portuguese:	coracao
Rumanian:	inima
Russian:	syertse
Spanish:	corazon
Swahili:	moyo
Swedish:	hjarta
Turkish:	kalb

Talk About It

Interview people from other countries and find out as many ways to say *friend* or *love* as you can.

Map It

Create a world of hearts by writing the correct word for *heart*, *friend* and/or *love* in as many countries as you can on a world map.

Challenge

See if you can figure out how the words in the list above are pronounced.

From Pumpkin Time to Valentines. Copyright 1994. Susan Ohanian. Teacher Ideas Press, P. O. Box 6633, Englewood, CO 80155.

Happy Birthday Valentine

Read About It

Jamake Highwater, George Shannon, and Paul Zelinsky were born on Valentine's Day.

Here are some other February birthdays:

February 7	Laura Ingalls Wilder
February 9	Dick Gackenbach
February 10	Elaine Konigsburg
	Stephen Gammell
February 11	Jane Yolen
February 12	Judy Blume
	David Small
	Chris Conover
February 15	Norman Bridwell
February 21	Jim Aylesworth
February 25	Cynthia Voigt

Read a book written and/or illustrated by these authors and artists. As your book report, create a valentine that would mean something special to this author/artist. For example, if you read Paul Zelinsky's *Rumpelstiltskin*, you might make his valentine out of gold foil.

From Pumpkin Time to Valentines. Copyright 1994. Susan Ohanian. Teacher Ideas Press, P. O. Box 6633, Englewood, CO 80155.

Once Upon a Time

Think About It

What if Goldilocks sent a valentine to the Three Bears. What might she say? What would their valentine to her say? Think of some other fairy tale characters. Create valentines they might send to each other.

From Pumpkin Time to Valentines. Copyright 1994. Susan Ohanian. Teacher Ideas Press, P. O. Box 6633, Englewood, CO 80155.

Mother Goose Valentines

Read About It

These Mother Goose rhymes have been changed into Valentine rhymes.

Jack Sprat could eat no fat,
His wife could eat no lean,
So they baked a valentine pie
And licked the platter clean.

Little Miss Muffet
Sat on a tuffet,
Writing her valentines.
Along came a spider
Who sat down beside her
And said, "Will you be mine?"

Write About It

Try giving a valentine theme to some Mother Goose rhymes. Here are the beginnings of some famous rhymes to help you get started. See how you can finish them.

Little Bo-peep has lost her valentines,

And doesn't know where to find them.

_____

_____.

There was an old woman who lived in a shoe.

She had so many valentines she didn't know what to do.

_____

_____.

From Pumpkin Time to Valentines. Copyright 1994. Susan Ohanian. Teacher Ideas Press, P. O. Box 6633, Englewood, CO 80155.

More Mother Goose Valentines

Write About It

Finish these valentine Mother Goose rhymes.

> Jack and Jill
>
> Went up the hill,
>
> To fetch a valentine.
>
> _____
>
> _____
>
> _____.

> Old Mother Hubbard
>
> Went to the cupboard
>
> To fetch her poor dog a valentine.
>
> But when she got there,
>
> _____
>
> _____
>
> _____.

Challenge

Turn another Mother Goose rhyme into a valentine rhyme.

From Pumpkin Time to Valentines. Copyright 1994. Susan Ohanian. Teacher Ideas Press, P. O. Box 6633, Englewood, CO 80155.

A Historic Happy Birthday

Read About It

Find out about someone famous born in February. Based on what you know about his or her life, create a special valentine for this person.

Here are some famous birthdays. You can use these or find others.

February 4   Charles Lindbergh
February 5   Hank Aaron
February 6   Babe Ruth
February 11   Thomas Edison
February 12   Abraham Lincoln
February 15   Galileo
February 22   George Washington
February 24   Wilhelm Grimm
February 25   Pierre Auguste Renoir

From Pumpkin Time to Valentines. Copyright 1994. Susan Ohanian. Teacher Ideas Press, P. O. Box 6633, Englewood, CO 80155.

A Newspaper Meal

Think About It

Plan a valentine's meal from the grocery ads in your newspaper. Be inventive. You can invent food combinations but each food should have something red in it (marshmallow pizza or pineapple spaghetti, for example).

Extra Credit

Figure out the cost of the meal you invent.

Write About It

Write an invitation for your valentine meal.
Invite whomever you wish.
Design a menu and an invitation.

From Pumpkin Time to Valentines. Copyright 1994. Susan Ohanian. Teacher Ideas Press, P. O. Box 6633, Englewood, CO 80155.

Names in the News

Think About It

Celebrate the real message of Valentine's Day by sending a friendly and helpful message to your community. Cut out two stories from the newspaper about problems in your community. Talk over these problems with a buddy reader. Choose one of them and with your buddy reader make a list of ways you think people might solve or at least improve the problem.

Choose a name in the news (such as mayor, city council member, business or labor leader) and with your buddy write that person a letter with your suggestions for improvement. Remember that a librarian can help you find addresses for mailing letters.

From Pumpkin Time to Valentines. Copyright 1994. Susan Ohanian. Teacher Ideas Press, P. O. Box 6633, Englewood, CO 80155.

Friendship

Think About It

Talk with two or three other students. With them, make a list of suggestions you have to make your classroom a friendlier place. Be specific. Share your list with the rest of the class. You might want to make a poster.

From Pumpkin Time to Valentines. Copyright 1994. Susan Ohanian. Teacher Ideas Press, P. O. Box 6633, Englewood, CO 80155.

More Names in the News

Read About It

Read the newspaper with the idea of choosing a valentine from one of the stories. You can choose someone famous or someone not-so-famous who you feel would appreciate your message. Create a valentine for that person . . . and send it! If you don't know where to mail your valentine, try visiting or phoning the reference desk of a city or university library for help.

From Pumpkin Time to Valentines. Copyright 1994. Susan Ohanian. Teacher Ideas Press, P. O. Box 6633, Englewood, CO 80155.

And More Names in the News

Think About It

From the newspaper cut at least two stories about problems in this country. Share your stories with a buddy reader. Choose one problem and talk about ways people might improve things. Make a list of things children might do to help. After you have made your list of suggestions, choose the name of a national leader you have read about in the news. Send that person your suggestions. Remember that a librarian can help you find the address to mail your letter.

From Pumpkin Time to Valentines. Copyright 1994. Susan Ohanian. Teacher Ideas Press, P. O. Box 6633, Englewood, CO 80155.

Valentine Mixups

Think About It

Homophones sound alike when you say them but have very different meanings. They can be used to make jokes and riddles.

Here's an example: the title of Fred Gwynne's book *A Chocolate Moose for Dinner* is a joke because the kind of chocolate you eat is spelled *mousse*. If you find a *moose* in your kitchen, you'd better drop your fork and call the game warden—fast!

Write About It

Use some of these homophones to create silly valentine's messages or riddles. Notice that the message makes sense. It's the picture that gives it a double meaning and makes it funny.

Here's a sample valentine message:
I'll give you every hair on my head if you will be mine.

cheap/cheep	chews/choose	dear/deer
you/ewe	hart/heart	horse/hoarse
toes/tows	leak/leek	crawl/kraal
lair/layer	tear/tier	liter/leader
flower/flour	night/knight	grease/Greece

From Pumpkin Time to Valentines. Copyright 1994. Susan Ohanian. Teacher Ideas Press, P. O. Box 6633, Englewood, CO 80155.

More Valentine Mixups

Read About It

Here are some more homophones. They are words that sound the same but have very different meanings. You can use homophones to create riddles. Here's a sample homophone valentine riddle:

Why are concerts the most popular place for valentine's parties?
(Because there are sacks-full of hearts.)

Write About It

It's your turn. Study these homophones and write a valentine riddle.

lion/lyin'	links/lynx	locks/lox
read/red	rain/reign/rein	toad/towed/toed
vein/vane/vain	wail/whale	wait/weight
marry/merry	carat/carrot	Chile/chili/chilly
gnu/new	odder/otter	bear/bare

From Pumpkin Time to Valentines. Copyright 1994. Susan Ohanian. Teacher Ideas Press, P. O. Box 6633, Englewood, CO 80155.

Still More Valentine Mixups

Read About It

Sometimes the same word has different meanings. An example is *tank*.

> People keep fish in a tank.
> Soldiers use tanks.
> People wear tank tops in the summer.

Sometimes all meanings of the word are pronounced the same way. Sometimes they are not. Take a look at *sow*, for example.

Sometimes a word has a different meaning in slang. *Bread*, for example, usually means something to eat. But in slang talk it can also mean money.

Check out some meanings of these words and create a silly valentine or a clever valentine riddle.

cob	row	drawers
pipe	sow	bass
dough	bread	bow

From Pumpkin Time to Valentines. Copyright 1994. Susan Ohanian. Teacher Ideas Press, P. O. Box 6633, Englewood, CO 80155.

Valentine Riddles

Read About It

Study these riddles and see if you can figure out how they are made. Think about how specific words and word twists make them funny.

What did one frog say to the other?
    Hoppy Valentine's!

What did one toad say to the other?
    Don't "froget" to be my Valentine.

What did one valentinosaur say to the other?
    Without you I'd be extinct.

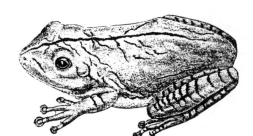

What did one owl say to another?
    Give a hoot! Be my Valentine.

Write About It

Turn these questions into valentine riddles. Share your answers with a buddy reader. If your answers are different, that's fine. There are many possible answers.

What did one ostrich say to another?

What did one camel say to another?

What did one cat say to another?

What did one elephant say to another?

What did one turtle say to another?

What did one chicken say to another?

From Pumpkin Time to Valentines. Copyright 1994. Susan Ohanian. Teacher Ideas Press, P. O. Box 6633, Englewood, CO 80155.

Antsy for You

Read About It

Poet and artist James Marsh draws an ape in his book *From the Heart* and says,

> My mouth's agape, I'm going ape,
> From your love there's no escape.

Can you think of any other words with *ape* in them?

In *There's an Ant in ANThony*, Bernard Most finds lots of words containing Ant, and illustrates them. In *ANTICS!* Cathi Hepworth finds lots of harder words containing ant, and her illustrations are spectacular.

Think About It

Try coming up with some other animal names and then find words that contain those names. Once you have your list you are well on your way to creating a great Animal Valentine Message.

Example: I'm getting ANTsy to be your valentine.

From Pumpkin Time to Valentines. Copyright 1994. Susan Ohanian. Teacher Ideas Press, P. O. Box 6633, Englewood, CO 80155.

Thumb-body Loves You!

Directions: Let your thumbprint be your guide to creating a valentine message. Here's a sample.

Thumb body Loves You!

From Pumpkin Time to Valentines. Copyright 1994. Susan Ohanian. Teacher Ideas Press, P. O. Box 6633, Englewood, CO 80155.

Halloween Bibliography

Pattern Stories

Ahlberg, Allan, and Janet Ahlberg, *Funnybones* (Mulberry, 1990).
Ahlberg, Allan, and Andre Amstutz, *Funnybones: The Black Cat* (Greenwillow, 1990).
————. *Funnybones: The Ghost Train* (Greenwillow, 1992; Mulberry, 1992).
————. *Funnybones: The Pet Shop* (Greenwillow, 1990).
————. *Funnybones: Skeleton Crew* (Greenwillow, 1992; Mulberry, 1992).
Brown, Marc, *Arthur's Halloween* (Joy Street pb, no date).
————. *Witches Four* (Parents Magazine Press; Putnam, 1980).
Brown, Ruth, *A Dark Dark Tale* (Dial, 1981; Pied Piper, no date).
Bunting, Eve, *In the Haunted House,* illus. Susan Meddaugh (Clarion, 1990).
————. *Scary, Scary Halloween,* illus. Jan Brett (Ticknor & Fields, 1986; Clarion, pb no date).
Cartwright, Pauline, *If I Were a Witch,* illus. Jan Van der Voo (The Wright Group, no date).
Enderle, Judith Ross, and Stephanie Gordon Tessler, *Six Creepy Sheep* (Caroline House, 1992).
Martin, Bill Jr., and John Archambault, *The Magic Pumpkin,* illus. Robert J. Lee (Henry Holt, 1989).
————. *The Ghost-Eye Tree,* illus. Ted Rand (Henry Holt, 1985; Owlet, 1988).
McNaughton, Colin, *Guess Who's Just Moved in Next Door?* (Random, 1991).
Silverman, Erica, *Big Pumpkin,* illus. S. D. Schindler (Macmillan, 1992).
Thompson, Carol, *Hide and Ghost Seek* (Platt & Munk, 1992).
Treece, Henry, *The Magic Wood,* illus. Barry Moser (HarperCollins, 1992).

Early Grades

Adams, Adrienne, *A Halloween Happening* (Scribner's, 1981, Aladdin pb,1991).
————. *A Woggle of Witches* (Macmillan, 1982).
Adler, David, *I Know I'm a Witch,* illus. Sucie Stevenson (Henry Holt, 1988; Owlet pb, 1990).
Alexander, Sue, *Who Goes Out on Halloween?* illus. G. Brian Karas (Bantam, 1990).
Allard, Harry, *Bumps in the Night,* illus. James Marshall (Doubleday, 1979; Bantam 1984).
Asch, Frank, *Popcorn* (Parents, 1979; Crown, no date).
Barton, Byron, *Hester* (Greenwillow, 1975; Mulberry, 1989).
Bender, Robert, *A Little Witch Magic* (Henry Holt, 1992).
Bennett, Jill, *Teeny Tiny,* illus. Tomie dePaola (Putnam, 1986).
Bentley, Nancy, *I've Got Your Nose!,* illus. Don Madden (Doubleday, 1991).
Bond, Felicia, *The Halloween Performance* (Harper, 1983).
Bridwell, Norman, *Clifford's Halloween* (Scholastic, 1970).
Brunhoff, Laurent de, *Babar and the Ghost,* easy-to-read version (Random pb,1981).
Bunting, Eve, *Ghost's Hour, Spook's Hour,* illus. Donald Carrick (Clarion pb, 1987).
Calmenson, Stephanie, *The Little Witch Sisters,* illus. R. W. Alley (Parents Magazine Press/Grosset, 1989; 1990 pb).
Carlson, Nancy, *Harriet's Halloween Candy* (Carolrhoda, 1982; Puffin, 1984).
————. *Louanne Pig in Witch Lady* (Carolrhoda, 1985; Puffin, 1986).
Carlson, Natalie Savage, *Spooky and the Bad Luck Raven,* illus. Andrew Glass (Lothrop, 1988).
————. *Spooky and the Ghost Cat,* illus. Andrew Glass (Lothrop, 1985).
Cassedy, Sylvia, *The Best Cat Suit of All,* illus. Rosekrans Hoffman (Dial, 1991).
Christelow, Eileen, *Jerome and the Witchcraft Kids* (Clarion pb, 1988).
Civardi, Annie, *The Wacky Book of Witches,* illus. Graham Philpot (Scholastic, 1992).
Cleary, Beverly, "Night of the Jack-O'-Lantern" in *Ramona and Her Father* (Morrow, 1977).
Cohen, Miriam, *The Real-Skin Rubber Monster Mask,* illus. Lillian Hoban (Greenwillow, 1990).
Cole, Joanna, *Bony-Legs* (Scholastic, 1983).
————. *Monster Manners,* illus. Jared Lee (Scholastic, 1985).
Coombs, Patricia, *Dorrie* series (Lothrop).
Cuyler, Margery, *Sir William and the Pumpkin Monster,* illus. Marsha Winburn (Henry Holt, 1984).
Davis, Maggie, *Rickety Witch,* illus. Kay Chorao (Holiday, 1984).

DeLage, Ida, *The Old Witch Series* (Chelsea).

Devlin, Wende, and Harry Devlin, *Cranberry Halloween* (Four Winds, 1982, Aladdin, 1990).

Dillon, Jana, *Jeb Scarecrow's Pumpkin Patch* (Houghton, 1992).

Donnelly, Liza, *Dinosaur Halloween* (Scholastic, 1987).

Enderle, Judith Ross, and Stephanie Gordon Tessler, *Six Creepy Sheep*, illus. John O'Brien (Caroline House, 1992).

Eyles, Heather, *Well I Never!* illus. Tony Ross (Overlook Press, 1990).

Fox, Mem, *Guess What?* illus. Vivienne Goodman (Harcourt Brace Jovanovich, 1990).

Freeman, Don, *Space Witch* (Viking, 1979).

Gage, Wilson, *Mrs. Gaddy and the Ghost*, illus. Marilyn Hafner (Greenwillow, 1979; Mulberry, 1991).

Galdone, Joanna, *The Tailypo: A Ghost Story*, illus. Paul Galdone (Seabury Press, 1977; Clarion pb, no date).

Gantos, Jack, *Rotten Ralph's Trick or Treat!* illus. Nicole Rubel (Houghton pb, 1986).

Gibbons, Gail, *Halloween* (Holiday, 1984).

Greenaway, Frank, *Eyewitness Juniors: Amazing Bats* (Knopf, 1991).

Guthrie, Donna, *The Witch Who Lives Down the Hall*, illus. Amy Schwartz (Harcourt Brace Jovanovich, 1985).

Hautzig, Deborah, *Little Witch's Big Night*, illus. Marc Brown (Random, 1984).

Herman, Emily, *Hubknuckles*, illus. Deborah Kogan Ray (Crown, 1985).

Himmelman, John, *Amanda and the Witch Switch* (Viking, 1985; Puffin, 1987).

Hoban, Lillian, *Arthur's Halloween Costume,* (Harper, 1984).

Hollyman, Sonia, *Mona the Vampire* (Delacorte, 1991).

Hughes, Frieda, *Getting Rid of Aunt Edna,* illus. Ed Levine (Harper, 1986).

Hurwitz, Johanna, *Nora and Mrs. Mind-Your-Own Business* (Morrow, 1977; Penguin, 1991).

Hutchins, Pat, *The Very Worst Monster* (Greenwillow, 1985; Mulberry, 1988).

Impey, Rose, *Creepies* series: *The Ankle Grabber; The Flat Man; Jumble Joan;* and *Scare Yourself to Sleep* (Barron's).

Johnston, Tony, *Four Scary Stories*, illus. Tomie dePaola (Putnam, 1978; pb 1988).

————. *The Soup Bone*, illus. Margot Tomes (Harcourt Brace Jovanovich, 1990).

————. *The Vanishing Pumpkin*, illus. Tomie dePaola (Putnam pb, 1983).

————. *The Witch's Hat*, illus. Margot Tomes (Putnam, 1984; Bantam, 1991).

Karlin, Nurit, *The Tooth Witch* (Harper, 1985).

Keats, Ezra Jack, *The Trip* (Greenwillow, 1978).

Keith, Eros, *Bedita's Bad Day* (Avon, 1985).

Kellogg, Steven, *The Mystery of the Flying Orange Pumpkin* (Dial, 1980).

Kraus, Robert, *How Spider Saved Halloween* (Dutton, 1980).

Kroll, Steven, *The Biggest Pumpkin Ever*, illus. Jeri Bassett (Scholastic, 1984).

Kunhardt, Edith, *Trick or Treat* (Greenwillow, 1988).

Leedy, Loreen, *The Dragon Halloween Party* (Holiday, 1986).

Low, Alice, *The Witch Who Was Afraid of Witches*, illus. Karen Gundersheimer (Pantheon, 1978; Harper Trophy, 1990).

————. *Zena and the Witch Circus*, illus. Laura Cornell (Dial, 1990).

Madsen, Ross Martin, *Perry Winkle and the Book of Magic Spells*, illus. Dirk Zimmer (Dial, 1986, pb 1988).

McAllister, Angela, *Nesta the Little Witch*, illus. Susie Jenkin-Pearce (Viking, 1990).

McNaughton, Colin, *Guess Who's Just Moved In Next Door?* (Random, 1991).

Manushkin, Fran, *Be Brave, Baby Rabbit*, illus. Diane De Groat (Crown, 1990).

Marshall, Edward, *Space Case*, illus. James Marshall (Dial, 1980).

Meddaugh, Susan, *The Witches' Supermarket* (Houghton, 1991).

Meyrick, Kathryn, *Hazel's Healthy Hallowe'en* (Child's Play, 1987).

Miller, Edward, *The Curse of Claudia* (Crown, 1989).

Mooser, Stephen, *The Ghost with the Halloween Hiccups*, illus. Tomie dePaola (Watts, 1977).

O'Connor, Jane, *Lulu Goes to Witch School*, illus. Emily Arnold McCully (Harper 1987; Harper Trophy, 1990).

Paul, Korky, and Valerie Thomas, *Winnie the Witch,* (Kane/Miller, 1987).

Pearson, Susan, *Porkchop's Halloween,* illus. Rick Brown (Simon & Schuster, 1988).

Pinkwater, Daniel, *Wempires* (Macmillan, 1991).

Prager, Annabelle, *The Spooky Halloween Party*, illus. Tomie dePaola (Pantheon, 1981).

Rose, David, *It Hardly Seems Like Halloween* (Lothrop, 1983).

Rosenberg, Liz, *Monster Mama*, illus. Stephen Gammell (Philomel, 1993).

Ross, Pat, *M & M and the Halloween Monster*, illus. Marylin Hafner (Viking, 1991).

Schertle, Alice, *Hob Goblin and the Skeleton,* illus. Katherine Coville (Lothrop, 1982).

Schubert, Ingrid, and Dieter Schubert, *Little Big Feet* (Lamniscaat v.b. 1986; Carolrhoda, 1990).

Schwartz, Alvin, *Ghosts! Ghostly Tales from Folklore,* illus. Victoria Chess (Harper, 1991).

Schwarz, Alvin, reteller, *In a Dark, Dark Room and Other Scary Stories,* illus. Dirk Zimmer (Harper, 1984; Harper Trophy, 1985).

Sharmat, Marjorie Weinman, *Nate the Great and the Halloween Hunt* (Coward-McCann, 1989).

Smith, Maggie, *There's a Witch Under the Stairs* (Lothrop, 1991).

Stevenson, James, *Emma* (Greenwillow, 1985).

———. *That Terrible Halloween Night* (Greenwillow, 1980; Mulberry, 1990).

———. *Yuck!* (Greenwillow, 1984).

Thompson, Carol, *Hide and Ghost Seek,* illus. Margaret Hartelius (Platt & Munk, 1992).

Titherington, Jeanne, *Pumpkin Pumpkin* (Greenwillow, 1986; Mulberry, 1990).

Tresselt, Alvin, *Autumn Harvest,* illus. Roger Duvoisin (Lothrop, 1951; Mulberry, 1990).

Updike, David, *An Autumn Tale,* illus. Robert Andrew Parker (Pippin, 1988).

Van Allsburg, Chris, *The Widow's Broom* (Houghton Mifflin, 1992).

Viorst, Judith, *My Mama Says There Aren't Any Zombies, Ghosts, Vampires, Creatures, Demons, Monsters, Fiends, Goblins, or Things,* illus. Kay Chorao (Atheneum, 1973).

Wahl, Jan, *Dracula's Cat and Frankenstein's Dog,* illus. Kay Chorao (Prentice- Hall, 1978; Simon and Schuster, 1990).

Williams, Linda, *The Little Old Lady Who Was Not Afraid of Anything,* illus. Megan Lloyd (Crowell, 1986).

Wiseman, Bernard, *Halloween with Morris and Boris* (Dodd, Mead, 1975; Scholastic, no date).

Wojciechowski, Susan, *The Best Halloween of All,* illus. Susan Meddaugh (Crown, 1992).

Wyllie, Stephen, *Ghost Train: A Spooky Hologram Book,* illus. Brian Lee (Dial, 1992).

Ziefert, Harriet, *Who Can Boo the Loudest?* illus. Claire Schumacher (Harper, 1990).

Zimmer, Dirk, *The Trick-or-Treat Trap* (Harper, 1982).

Zolotow, Charlotte, *A Tiger Called Thomas,* illus. Catherine Stock (Lothrop, 1988).

Middle Grades

Balian, Lorna, *Humbug Potion: An ABC Cipher* (Abingdon Press, 1984).

Barth, Edna, *Witches, Pumpkins, and Grinning Ghosts: The Story of the Halloween Symbols* (Clarion, 1972; pb).

Battles, Edith, *The Witch in Room 6* (Harper, 1987).

Belairs, John, *The Dark Secret of Weatherend* (Bantam).

———. *The Mummy, the Will, and the Crypt* (Bantam).

Bird, Malcolm, *The Witch's Handbook* (David Booth Ltd., 1984; Aladdin, 1988).

Bradbury, Ray, *The Halloween Tree* (Knopf, 1972; 1988).

Bunting, Eve, *The Ghost Children* (Houghton, 1989; Bantam, 1991).

Cates, Emily, *Haunting with Louisa* series (Bantam).

Chetwin, Grace, *On All Hallows' Eve* (Lothrop, 1984).

Cohen, Daniel, *America's Very Own Ghosts,* illus. Alix Bernzy (Dodd, Mead, no date).

———. *Curses, Hexes and Spells* (Harper, 1974).

———. *Erni Cabat's Magical World of Monsters,* illus. Erni Cabat (Cobblehill, 1992).

———. *Monsters You Never Heard Of* (Dodd, Mead, 1980; Archway, 1991).

Cole, Joanna, and Stephanie Calmenson, compilers, *The Scary Book,* illus. by Chris Demarest, Marilyn Hirsh, Arnold Lobel, and Dirk Zimmer (Morrow, 1991).

Colville, Bruce, *The Ghost in the Big Brass Bed* (Bantam, 1991).

———. *The Ghost in the Third Row* (Bantam, 1991).

———. *The Ghost Wore Gray* (Bantam, 1990).

Dadey, Debbie, and Marcia Thornton Jones, *Vampires Don't Wear Polka Dots—or Do They?* (Scholastic, 1990).

Dahl, Roald, *The Witches,* illus. Quentin Blake (Farrar, Straus, 1983, Puffin, 1985).

Deem, James *How to Find a Ghost* (Avon, 1988).

DeFelice, Cynthia, *The Dancing Skeleton,* illus. Robert Andrew Parker (Macmillan, 1989).

Dixon, Franklin, *The Hardy Boys Ghost Stories* (Minstrel, 1987).

Estes, Eleanor, *The Witch Family* (Harcourt Brace Jovanovich, 1960; pb 1990).

Fleischman, Sid, *The Ghost in the Noonday Sun* (Morrow, 1986; Scholastic, 1991).

Flora, James, *Grandpa's Ghost Stories* (Aladdin pb, 1978).

Gilden, Mel, *Welcome to P.S. 13 "Fifth Grade Monster"* series (Avon).

Gilligan, Shannon, *The Haunted Swamp: Our Secret Gang #2* (Bantam, 1992).

Graham, Alastair, *Full Moon Soup: Or the Fall of the Hotel Splendide* (Dial, 1991).

Greenberg, Martin H., and Charles Waugh, selectors, *A Newbery Halloween* (Delacorte Press, 1993).

Greene, Carol, *The Thirteen Days of Halloween* (Childrens, 1983).

Hamilton, Virginia, *Willie Bea and the Time the Martians Landed* (Greenwillow, 1983).

Haynes, Betsy, *The Witches of Wakeman: The Fabulous Five #20* (Bantam, 1992).

Hawkins, Colin, and an old witch, *Witches* (Granada, 1981; Silver Burdett, 1985).

Hawkins, Colin, and Jacqui Hawkins, and a ghost writer, *Spooks* (Granada, 1983; Silver Burdett, 1985).

Hawkins, Colin, et al., *Vampires* (Granada, 1982; Silver Burdett, 1985).

Haywood, Carolyn, *Halloween Treats* (Morrow, 1981; Troll, no date).

Helldorfer, M. C., *Spook House* (Bradbury, 1989).

Herda, D. J., *Halloween* (Franklin Watts, 1983).

Herzig, Alison Crogin, and Jane Laurence Mali, *Mystery on October Road* (Viking, 1991).

Hiser, Constance, *Ghosts in Fourth Grade* (Holiday House, 1991).

Howe, James, *Harold & Chester in Scared Silly: A Halloween Treat,* illus. Leslie Morrill (Morrow, 1989).

Irving, Washington, *The Legend of Sleepy Hollow,* illus. Michael Garland (Caroline House, 1992).

Jacques, Brian, *Seven Strange & Ghostly Tales* (Philomel, 1991).

Keene, Carolyn, *Nancy Drew Ghost Stories* (Minstrel, 1987).

Kroll, Steven, *Branigan's Cat and the Halloween Ghost,* illus. Carolyn Ewing (Holiday, 1990).

Leach, Maria, *The Thing at the Foot of the Bed and Other Scary Tales* (William Collins, 1959; Dell Yearling, 1977).

Levy, Elizabeth, *Dracula is a Pain in the Neck,* illus. Mordicai Gerstein (Harper, 1983).

———. *Frankenstein Moved in on the Fourth Floor,* illus. Mordicai Gerstein (Harper, 1979).

———. *Something Queer at the Haunted School* (Dell Yearling).

Limberg, Peter, *Weird! The Complete Book of Halloween Words* (Bradbury, 1989).

Lively, Penelope, *The Ghost of Thomas Kempe* (Dutton, 1973; Berkeley).

———. *The Revenge of Samuel Stokes* (Dutton, 1981).

———. *Uninvited Ghosts and Other Stories* (Dutton, 1985).

MacDonald, George, *The Princess and the Goblin,* various illus. (Putnam, 1985; Morrow, 1986; Eerdmans, 1987).

Markham, Marion, *The Halloween Candy Mystery,* illus. Emily Arnold McCully (Houghton, 1982, Avon, 1990).

Martin, Ann M. *Ma and Pa Dracula,* illus. Dirk Zimmer (Holiday, 1989).

Meyers, Susan, *P. J. Clover, Private Eye: The Case of the Halloween Hoot* (Lodestar, 1990).

Miller, Judi, *Confessions of an Eleven-Year-Old Ghost* (Bantam, 1991).

———. *Ghost a la Mode* (Bantam, 1991).

———. *Ghost in My Soup* (Bantam, 1991).

———. *A Vampire Named Murray* (Bantam, 1991).

Montresor, Beni, *The Witches of Venice* (Doubleday, 1989).

Mooser, Stephen, *My Halloween Boyfriend,* illus. George Ulrich (Dell Yearling, 1989); other titles in the Creepy Creature Club series include: *Monsters in the Outfield, Monster Holiday, The Fright-Face Contest; That's So Funny, I Forgot to Laugh, Monster of the Year, Secrets of Scary Fun, The Night of the Vampire Kitty.*

———. *The Hitchiking Vampire* (Delacorte, 1989).

Murphy, Jill, *The Worst Witch* (Puffin, 1978; Viking Kestrel, 1988).

Ormondroyd, Edward, *Time at the Top* (Bantam, 1963).

Packard, Edward, *Ghost Hunter (Choose Your Own Adventure #52)* (Bantam, 1992).

Parker, Steve, *Skeleton: Eyewitness Books* (Knopf, 1988).

Pascal, Francine, *Sweet Valley Trick or Treat* (Bantam, 1990).

Peel, John, *Foul Play* series (Puffin).

Place, Marian, *The First Astrowitches* (Dodd, Mead, 1984; Avon, 1985).

———. *The Resident Witch* (Avon, 1986).

———. *The Witch Who Saved Halloween* (Avon, 1986).

Polidori, John, *The Vampire,* adapted by Les Martin (Random pb, 1989).

Polisar, Barry Louis, *The Haunted House Party* (Rainbow Morning Music, 1987).

Razzi, Jim *Spine Chillers* series (Grosset & Dunlap, 1990).

Regan, Dian Curtis, *Jilly's Ghost* (Avon, 1990).

Roos, Stephen, *Love Me, Love My Werewolf* (Delacorte, 1991).

Schulman, Janet, *Jack the Bum and the Halloween Handout,* illus. James Stevenson (UNICEF, 1977).

Schwartz, Alvin, collector, *More Scary Stories to Tell in the Dark,* illus. Stephen Gammell (Lippincott, 1984).

———. *Scary Stories to Tell in the Dark,* illus. Stephen Gammell (Lippincott, 1981; pb).

Schwartz, Alvin, reteller, *Scary Stories: More Tales to Chill Your Bones,* illus. Stephen Gammell (Harper pb, 1991).

126

Sommer-Bodenburg, Angela, *If You Want to Scare Yourself,* illus. Helga Spiess (Otto Maier Verlag, 1984; Lippincott, 1989).

————. *The Vampire in Love* (Dial, 1991).

————. *The Vampire on the Farm* (Andersen Press, 1985, Minstrel pb, 1990). Other titles in this series from Minstrel include: *My Friend, the Vampire* and *The Vampire Moves In.*

————. *The Vampire Takes a Trip* (Minstrel 1991).

Stine, Megan, and H. William Stine, *Jeffrey and the Fourth-Grade Ghost* series (Fawcett Columbine).

————. *Jeffrey and the Third-Grade Ghost* series (Fawcett Columbine).

Udry, Janice May, *Glenda,* illus. Marc Simont (Harper, 1969; Trophy, 1991).

Ure, Jean, *Wizard in Wonderland* (Candlewick, 1991).

Van Allsburg, Chris, *The Widow's Broom* (Houghton Mifflin, 1992).

Weiss, Ellen, and Mel Friedman, *The Adventures of Ratman,* illus. Dirk Zimmer (Random House Stepping Stone, 1990).

Wippersberg, W. J. M., *Bad Times for Ghosts* (Benziger Verlag, 1984; Harcourt Brace Jovanovich, 1986).

Wright, Betty Ren, *The Ghost of Popcorn Hill* (Holiday, 1993).

Anthologies

Bauer, Caroline Feller, *Halloween: Stories and Poems,* illus. Peter Sis (Lippincott, 1989).

Cecil, Laura, compiler, *Boo! Stories to Make You Jump,* illus. Emma Chichester Clark (Greenwillow, 1990).

Hodges, Margaret, compiler, *Hauntings: Ghosts and Ghouls from Around the World* (Little, Brown, 1991).

Hunt, Roderick, *Ghosts, Witches, and Things Like That* (Oxford University, 1984).

MacDonald, Margaret Read, *When the Lights Go Out: Scary Tales to Tell* (H. W. Wilson, 1988).

McKissack, Patricia, *The Dark-Thirty: Southern Tales of the Supernatural,* illus. Brian Pinkney (Knopf, 1992).

San Souci, Robert D., reteller, *Short & Shivery,* illus. Katherine Coville (Doubleday, 1987).

Schwartz, Alvin, reteller, *Scary Stories to Tell in the Dark,* illus. Stephen Gammell (Lippincott, 1981).

Westall, Robert, compiler, *Ghost Stories* (Kingfisher, 1993).

Yolen, Jane, and Martin H. Greenberg, ed., *Things That Go Bump in the Night* (Harper, 1989).

————. *Vampires* (Harper, 1991).

Young, Richard, and Judy Dockrey, *Favorite Scary Stories of American Children* (August House, pb 1990).

Zimmerman, Howard, Seymour Reit, and Barbara Brenner, eds., *The Bank Street Book of Creepy Tales* (Pocket Books, 1989).

Poetry

Beisner, Monika, *Secret Spells & Curious Charms* (Farrar, Straus & Giroux, 1985).

Bennett, Jill, collector, *Spooky Poems* (Little, Brown, 1989).

cummings, e. e. *Hist Whist,* illus. Deborah Kogan Ray (Crown, 1989).

Evans, Dilyn, compiler, *Monster Soup and Other Spooky Poems,* illus. Jacqueline Rogers (Scholastic, 1992).

Heide, Florence Parry, *Grim and Ghastly Goings-on,* illus. Victoria Chess (Lothrop, 1992).

Hopkins, Lee Bennett, selector, *Creatures,* illus. Stella Ormai (Harcourt Brace Jovanovich, 1985; Voyager, 1990).

Katz, Bobbi, selector, *Ghosts and Goose Bumps: Poems to Chill Your Bones,* illus. Deborah Kogan Ray (Random House, pb 1991).

Livingston, Myra Cohn, selector, *Halloween Poems,* illus. Stephen Gammell (Holiday, 1989).

Merriam, Eve, *Halloween ABC,* illus. Lane Smith (Macmillan, 1987).

Ohuigin, Sean, *Monsters He Mumbled* (Black Moss Press/Firefly Books, 1989).

Prelutsky, Jack, *The Headless Horseman Rides Tonight* (Greenwillow, 1980; Mulberry, 1992).

————. *It's Halloween* (Greenwillow, 1977; Scholastic, no date).

Treece, Henry, *The Magic Wood,* illus. Barry Moser (HarperCollins, 1992).

Ulrich, George, *The Spook Matinee and Other Scary Poems for Kids* (Delacorte, 1992).

Wallace, Daisy, ed. *Ghost Poems,* illus. Tomie dePaola (Holiday, 1979; pb).

Yolen, Jane, *Best Witches: Poems for Halloween,* illus. Elise Primavera (Putnam, 1989).

Books for Games and Projects

Baker, James, *Halloween Magic* (Lerner, 1988).

Bolognese, Don, and Elaine Raphael, *The Way to Draw and Color Monsters* (Random House, pb 1991).
Burr, Daniella, *Don't Just Sit There! 50 Ways to Have a Nickelodeon Day* (Grosset and Dunlap, 1992).
Conaway, Judith, *Happy Haunting! Halloween Costumes You Can Make* (Troll, 1986).
Emberley, Ed, *Ed Emberley's Big Orange Drawing Book* (Little, Brown, 1980; pb).
Rayner, Shoo, *Gruesome Games: Twelve Great New Spine-Tingling Board Games* (Bedrick-Blackie, 1988).
Saunders, Richard, and Brian Mackness, *Horrogami: Spooky Paperfolding* (Sterling, 1992).
Speirs, John, *Ghostly Games* (Reader's Digest, 1991).
Stamper, Judith, *Halloween Holiday Grab Bag* (Troll, 1993).
West, Robin, *My Very Own Halloween: A Book of Cooking and Crafts* (Carolrhoda, 1992).

Lift the Flap and Other Moveable Books

Carter, David, *In a Dark, Dark Wood* (Simon and Schuster, 1991).
Gardner, Beau, *Whooo's a Fright on Halloween Night?* (Putnam, 1990).
Faulkner, Keith, *My New Neighbors,* illus. Jonathan Lambert (Harper, 1992).
Moseley, Keith, designer, *The Door Under the Stairs,* illus. Andy Everett-Stewart (Grosset, 1990).
————. *Some Bodies in the Attic,* illus. Andy Everett-Stewart (Grosset & Dunlap, 1990).
Paul, Korky, *The Pop-Up Book of Ghost Tales* (Harcourt Brace Jovanovich, 1991).
Pienkowski, Jan, *Haunted House* (Dutton).
Ziefert, Harriet, *Where's the Halloween Treat?* illus. Richard Brown (Puffin, 1985).
Ziefert, Harriet, and Mavis Smith, *In a Scary Old House* (Puffin, 1989).

Riddle and Joke Books

Adler, David, *The Twisted Witch and Other Spooky Riddles,* illus. Victoria Chess.
Cole, William, and Mike Thaler, *Monster Knock Knocks,* illus. Mike Thaler (Archway, 1982; Minstrel, 1988).
Fremont, Eleanor, *Jokes from the Crypt* (Random House, 1992).
Keller, Charles, *Count Draculations! Monster Riddles,* (Simon & Schuster, 1986).
Maestro, Giulio, *Halloween Howls* (Dutton, 1992).
Phillips, Louis, *Haunted House Jokes,* illus. James Marshall (Viking Kestrel, 1987).
Rosenbloom, Joseph, *The Funniest Haunted House Book Ever!* illus. Hans Wilhelm (Sterling, 1989).
————. *Ridiculous Nicholas Haunted House Riddles,* illus. Joyce Behr (Sterling, 1983).
————. *Spooky Riddles and Jokes,* illus. Sanford Hoffman (Sterling, 1987).
Seltzer, Meyer, ghostwriter, *Hide-and-Go-Shriek Monster Riddles* (Whitman, 1990).
Stein, Frank N., *1,000 Monster Jokes for Kids* (Ballantine, 1989).
Stine, Jovial Bob, *101 Silly Monster Jokes* (Scholastic, 1986).
Thaler, Mike, *Frankenstein's Pantyhose* (Avon, 1989).

Adult Resources

Bannatyne, Lesley Pratt, *Halloween: An American Holiday, An American History* (Facts On File, 1990).
Lorie, Peter, *Superstitions* (Simon & Schuster, 1992).

Valentine's Day Bibliography

Projects

Baker, James, *Valentine Magic* (Lerner, 1988).
Bohning, Gerry, Ann Phillips, and Sandra Bryant, *Literature on the Move: Making and Using Pop-Up and Lift-Flap Books* (Teacher Ideas Press, 1993).
Folmer, A. P., *Valentine Pop-Up Cards to Make Yourself* (Scholastic, 1991).
Irvine, Joan, *How to Make Pop-Ups* (Morrow, 1988).
————. *How To Make Super Pop-Ups* (Beech Tree, 1992).

Kennedy, Paul, *Fun with Hearts Stencils* (Dover, 1992).
————. *Fun with Valentine Stencils* (Dover, 1990).
Stamper, Judith, *Valentine: Holiday Grab Bag* (Troll, 1993).

Early Grades

Adams, Adrienne, *The Great Valentine's Day Balloon Race* (Scribner's, 1980; Aladdin, 1986).
Brown, Marc, *Arthur's Valentine* (Little, Brown, 1980; 1987).
Bond, Felicia, *Four Valentines in a Rainstorm* (Harper, 1983; 1990).
Buckley, Kate, *Love Notes* (Albert Whitman, 1989).
Bunting, Eve, *The Valentine Bears*, illus. Jan Brett (Houghton, 1983).
Cohen, Miriam, *Bee My Valentine!*, illus. Lillian Hoban (Greenwillow, 1978; Dell).
Devlin, Wende, and Harry, *Cranberry Valentine* (Macmillan, 1986).
Ehrlich, Fred, *A Valentine for Ms. Vanilla*, illus. Martha Gradisher (Viking, 1991).
Gibbons, Gail, *Valentine's Day* (Holiday, 1986).
Graham, Bob, *Crusher Is Coming!* (Viking, 1988).
Henkes, Kevin, *Chester's Way* (Greenwillow, 1988).
Hoban, Lillian, *Arthur's Great Big Valentine* (Harper, 1989).
Hurd, Thatcher, *Little Mouse's Big Valentine* (HarperCollins, 1990).
King, Larry, *Because of Lozo Brown*, illus. Amy Schwartz (Penguin, 1988; 1990).
Kraus, Robert, *How Spider Saved Valentine's Day* (Scholastic, 1985).
Krauss, Ruth, *I'll Be You and You Be Me*, illus. Maurice Sendak (Harper, 1954).
Kroll, Steven, *Will You Be My Valentine?* (Holiday, 1993).
Lexau, Joan, *Don't Be My Valentine*, illus. Syd Hoff (Harper, 1985).
Mariana, *Miss Flora McFlimsey's Valentine* (Lothrop, 1987).
Modell, Frank, *One Zillion Valentines* (Morrow, 1981; Greenwillow, 1987).
Murphy, Shirley Rousseau, *Valentine for a Dragon*, illus. Kay Chorao (Macmillan, 1984).
Nixon, Joan Lowery, *The Valentine Mystery* (Whitman, 1979).
Ross, Dave, *Little Mouse's Valentine* (Morrow, 1986).
Schweninger, Ann, *Valentine Friends* (Puffin, 1988; Scholastic, 1991).
Sharmat, Marjorie Weinman, *The Best Valentine in the World*, illus. Lilian Obligado (Holiday, 1982).
————. *The 329th Friend*, illus. Cyndy Szekeres (Four Winds, 1979; 1992).
Spinelli, Eileen, *Somebody Loves You, Mr. Hatch*, illus. Paul Yalowitz (Bradbury, 1991).
Stevenson, James, *Happy Valentine's Day, Emma!* (Greenwillow, 1987).
Walton, Marilyn Jeffers, *Sparky's Valentine Victory* (Raintree, 1983).
Watson, Clyde, *Valentine Foxes*, illus. Wendy Watson (Orchard, 1989; 1992).
Williams, Barbara, *A Valentine for Cousin Archie*, illus. Kay Chorao (Dutton, 1981).
Wittman, Sally, *The Boy Who Hated Valentine's Day*, illus. Chaya Burstein (Harper, 1987).
Zolotow, Charlotte, *Some Things Go Together*, illus. Karen Gundersheimer (Harper, 1969; 1983).

Middle Grades

Cohen, Barbara, *213 Valentines* (Henry Holt, 1991).
Giff, Patricia Reilly, *The Valentine Star* (Dell, 1985).
Goldman, Kelly, and Ronnie Davidson, *Sherlick Hound and the Valentine Mystery*, illus. Don Madden (Albert Whitman, 1989).
Herman, Charlotte, *Millie Cooper, Take a Chance* (Penguin, 1988; Puffin, 1990).
Markham, Marion, *The Valentine's Day Mystery* (Houghton Mifflin, 1992).
Milcsik, Margie, *Cupid Computer* (Aladdin, 1992).
Mooser, Stephen, *Crazy Mixed-Up Valentines* (Dell Young Yearling, 1991).
Peck, Robert Newton, *Soup In Love* (Delacorte, 1992).
Sabuda, Robert, *Saint Valentine* (Atheneum, 1992).
Smith, Janice Lee, *Nelson in Love: An Adam Joshua Valentine's Day Story*, illus. Dick Gackenbach (Harper, 1992).
Twohill, Maggie, *Valentine Frankenstein* (Bradbury, 1991).
Williams, Barbara, *A Valentine for Cousin Archie*, illus. Kay Chorao (Dutton, 1981).

Poetry and Word Study for All Ages

Ahlberg, Janet, and Allan Ahlberg, *The Clothes Horse and Other Stories* (Viking, 1987).

Black, Sonia, and Pat Brigandi, *Super Word Tricks* (Scholastic, 1989).

Espy, Willard, *A Children's Almanac of Words at Play* (Clarkson Potter, 1982).

Fraser, Betty, *First Things First: An Illustrated Collection of Sayings* (Harper, 1990).

Geringer, Laura, *Yours 'Til the Ice Cracks,* illus. Andrea Baruffi (Harper, 1992).

Gibbons, Gail, *Valentine's Day* (Holiday House, 1986).

Graham-Barber, Lynda, *Mushy! The Complete Book of Valentine Words* (Bradbury, 1991).

Gwynne, Fred, *A Chocolate Moose for Dinner* (Prentice-Hall, 1976).

———. *The King Who Rained* (Simon & Schuster, 1986).

———. *A Little Pigeon Toad* (Simon & Schuster, 1988).

———. *The Sixteen Hand Horse* (Simon & Schuster, 1980).

Hepworth, Cathi, *ANTICS!* (Putnam, 1992).

Hopkins, Lee Bennett, selector, *Good Morning to You, Valentine,* illus. Tomie dePaola (Harcourt Brace Jovanovich, 1976).

Kennedy, Richard, *Little Love Song,* illus. Petra Mathers (Knopf, 1992).

Krauss, Ruth, *Big and Little,* illus. Mary Szilagyi (Scholastic, 1987).

Livingston, Myra Cohn, *Valentine Poems,* illus. Patience Brewster (Holiday House, 1987).

Marsh, James, *From the Heart: Light-Hearted Verse* (Dial, 1993).

Most, Bernard, *There's an Ant in ANThony* (Morrow, 1980; 1992).

Prelutsky, Jack, *It's Valentine's Day,* illus. Yossi Abolafia (Greenwillow, 1983).

Terban, Marvin, *In a Pickle and Other Funny Idioms* (Clarion, 1983).

———. *Superdupers! Really Funny Real Words* (Clarion, 1989).

Warburg, Sandol Stoddard, *I Like You* (Houghton Mifflin, 1965).

Zolotow, Charlotte, *Some Things Go Together* (Harper, 1969; 1987).

Adult

Auchincloss, Louis, *Love Without Wings: Some Friendships in Literature and Politics* (Houghton Mifflin, 1991).

Bandreth, Gyles, *The Joy of Lex* (Morrow, 1980).

Brock, Suzanne, *Idiom's Delight* (Times Books, 1988).

Cobb, Nancy, *How They Met* (Turtle Bay Book, 1992).

Edmark, Tomima, *Kissing: Everything You Ever Wanted to Know* (Simon & Schuster, 1991).

Espy, Willard, *An Almanac of Words at Play* (Clarkson Potter, no date).

———. *Another Almanac of Words at Play* (Clarkson Potter, 1980).

Ewart, Neil, *Everyday Phrases: Their Origins and Meanings* (Blandford Press/Sterling, 1985).

Fraser, Antonia, *Love Letters* (Contemporary Books, 1989).

Geller, Linda Gibson, *Wordplay and Language Learning* (NCTE, 1985).

Golick, Margie, *Playing with Words* (Pembroke/Heinemann, 1987).

Makkai, et al., eds., *Dictionary of American Idioms* (Barron's, 1987).

Ohanian, Susan, *Go Fry Asparagus!* Poster & Teaching Guide (*Learning89,* September).

———. *Within the Forest* (SRA/Macmillan/McGraw-Hill, 1991).

———. *Word Play* (Springhouse, 1990).

Rosenthal, Peggy, and George Dardess, *Every Cliche in the Book* (Morrow, 1987).

About the Author

Susan Ohanian received her master's degree in English from University of California, Berkeley. She has written five books and over 200 articles for *Education Week*, *Phi Delta Kappan*, *English Journal*, *College English*, *Reading Teacher*, *Instructor*, and *Learning* and is frequently anthologized in education texts.

Susan is on the NCTE Language Arts Textbook Committee, CEE Executive Committee, and the IRA Intellectual Freedom Committee. She has won several writing awards from *English Journal* and *Educational Press*.

A longtime teacher, Susan is currently an education writer based in Schenectady, New York.